# *this i*

SECOND EDITION

# Ian Ithurralde • Anne Ramkaran

## Hodder & Stoughton
A MEMBER OF THE HODDER HEADLINE GROUP

Orders: please contact Bookpoint Ltd, 130 Milton Park, Abingdon, Oxon OX14 4SB. Telephone: (44) 01235 827720, Fax: (44) 01235 400454. Lines are open from 9.00–6.00, Monday to Saturday, with a 24 hour message answering service. Email address: orders@bookpoint.co.uk

*British Library Cataloguing in Publication Data*
A catalogue record for this title is available from The British Library

ISBN 0340 73809 X

First published 1999
Impression number    10  9  8  7  6  5  4
Year                            2005  2004  2003  2002

Typeset by Wearset, Boldon, Tyne and Wear.
Printed in Italy for Hodder & Stoughton Educational, a division of Hodder Headline Plc, 338 Euston Road, London NW1 3BH by Printer Trento.

# Contents

# Introduction

## ▮ *How to use this book*

This book is intended primarily for students following the National Curriculum Information Technology programmes of study at key stages three and four. It will also prove useful if you are following skills-based courses for GNVQ. Whether you are taught IT as a specialist subject, or you are set tasks in other subject areas, and whatever hardware or software you're using, there are some design skills which you need to learn, and some methods which work better than others. This book will show you how to produce effective IT solutions to problems and, by looking at various applications of IT, will give you an insight into the wider aspects of the use of IT and its impact on society.

You are not expected to sit down and read the whole book, or even to read the chapters in order. Each main type of package you are likely to need to use has at least one chapter devoted to it. When you have an IT task to carry out, find the chapter you need and read it carefully. You will learn what you can expect the software to do and also how to approach the task to get the best results.

You will not find specific instructions for different software packages as there isn't room to cover all the packages available in one book. We suggest that you keep a notebook with a section for each package you use. As you find out the exact commands needed for that package you can write them down for easy reference.

Throughout the book we have stressed the importance of design. You will get the best out of IT work by doing the design work first, working through all the steps suggested. At the end of most chapters there is a list of suggestions for tasks you might try. Further tasks and worksheets are available in the worksheet and CD-ROM pack.

There are questions throughout the book. Some of these are examination questions, others are short questions within the chapters. Try to do these short questions as you come to them. They will show whether you have understood what you have read.

Each time a new technical term is introduced it appears in **bold** type. All these terms are explained in the glossary at the back of the book. We have tried not to include lots of technical detail about computer systems and software. If you want to know more you should read *This is IT 2*, which covers all the additional work needed for GCSE Information Technology courses and gives you more detailed information on the applications of IT.

# Information and Data

## ■ *What is information?*

Here is a piece of information:

*The dog is fluffy.*

This information tells us something about the dog. Information is always about something. It always has a **context**. If we take away the context the information loses its meaning. The word 'fluffy' on its own doesn't tell us anything.

### PICTURES

We don't always provide information in words. The photograph on this page gives us the same information as the sentence above.

In some instances pictures can be more useful than words. For example, very young children can't read words but can learn to recognise pictures quite quickly.

### GRAPHS AND CHARTS

Information can also be provided in the form of a graph or a chart. This can show important trends more clearly than a table of numbers. In Figure 1.1 the graph shows much more clearly that the average temperature is generally going up during this period than the table does, even though the line does go up and down a little from month to month. Always remember that presenting information like this can be misleading.

*This picture gives us the same information as in the sentence – the dog is fluffy.*

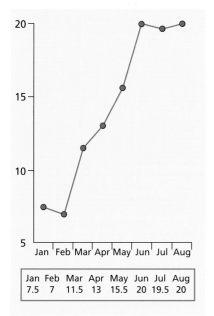

| Jan | Feb | Mar | Apr | May | Jun | Jul | Aug |
|-----|-----|-----|-----|-----|-----|-----|-----|
| 7.5 | 7 | 11.5 | 13 | 15.5 | 20 | 19.5 | 20 |

**Figure 1.1** *The data presented in the table is much more meaningful if it is presented in a graphical form.*

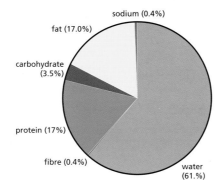

sodium (0.4%)
fat (17.0%)
carbohydrate (3.5%)
protein (17%)
fibre (0.4%)
water (61.%)

**Figure 1.2** *Pie chart to show what goes into a beefburger.*

You can make small changes look big, or disguise large changes by choosing the scales on a graph carefully.

A pie-chart (like the one in Figure 1.2) is a good way to show how something is divided up. In this example we can see what kinds of food we get when we eat a beefburger, and what proportion of each kind we are eating.

## SYMBOLS

Symbols can also be used to provide us with information. When we use symbols to get information across, we depend on the person who looks at them being able to understand the meaning of the symbols and interpret them correctly.

Look at Figure 1.3. These signs can give us information about roads, but only if we know what they mean. If we don't understand a symbol's meaning it provides no information to us. As long as we can understand them, symbols are a very good way of providing information quickly and effectively.

## SOUND

A great deal of the information we receive each day comes to us as sound – we are often told what to do, rather than being given written instructions. Your friends tell you where they have been and what they did. This kind of information is called **aural** information. It includes speech, music, and other kinds of noise.

**Q**

Write down five different ways in which you can give information.

For each of these ways, think of an example where people use it in everyday life. Is there a particular reason why the information is given in this way?

Why are symbols sometimes used instead of words?

**Figure 1.3** *The symbols in this figure can give us information about roads – but only if we understand them.*

# ■ *What is data?*

Computers do not store information, they store data. Data has no context, it is just numbers and has no meaning until it is given a context. The computer can't think for itself. It doesn't know (and doesn't care) if the data it stores is correct for the use it's going to be put to – it is up to the user to make sure that the correct data has been entered and that they use it correctly.

A computer stores all data as **binary numbers**, which are made up only of ones and zeros. For example, it stores the letter A as the binary number 01000001. Binary numbers like this can be used to represent letters, other characters (like * % ! or <), numeric values, **graphics** or sounds.

Here are some examples of data items which could be stored in a computer.

> 47
> Red
> 19/02/96
> −456

# Summary

- **Information** always has a **context**, and always has meaning for the person receiving it – for example the photograph on this page and Figure 1.4 contain information.

*Here the colour red gives us information.*

**Figure 1.4** *Here the number six gives us information.*

- **Data** has no context and is meaningless until a context is supplied – 'red' and '6' are data.

## SKILLS

When you have completed the work in this chapter you should be able to:

● Extract data from information.

● Work out what form of information to use for a task.

● Put data into a context.

## Questions

**1** Read this advertisement.

# FOR SALE:
### Four bedroom detached house in rural setting.
### Large landscaped gardens with fruit trees.
### £120,000.

Identify four data items that you might store in a computer file containing information on properties for sale.

**2** Match these three data items to the contexts in the sentences below:
£8.56
100
Green

**a** The computer has a hard disk which stores     megabytes.
**b** The door of the house is painted        .
**c** The bill for the meal was        .

For each data item, write a new sentence into which you could insert this item.

**3** Mrs. Brown is divorced with two children. She has recently returned to full-time education and is in the final year of a Science degree. She has taken out student loans of £5000. She regularly plays squash at the local sports centre. She does not have any credit cards. She rents a council house from her Local Authority.

**a** Using only the information given above, write down **four** facts about Mrs. Brown which are likely to be stored in a computer database.
**b** Explain clearly the difference between information and data.

(NEAB)

4 Information can be presented in many forms. A common one is text. Two other forms of presenting information are symbols and graphs/charts. For **each one**, give an example of a situation where it is used and give a reason why it might be better than text **in that situation**. (NEAB)

5 Information can be presented in different **forms**. For example, **sound** is used when a teacher tells a pupil what to do at the start of a lesson.
State **two other different forms** of information and for each, give an example of its use. (NEAB)

# Handling Information

## ■ *Why use a computer to handle information?*

Information has always been stored in some way – until recently, in schools, hospitals, shops and offices, lots of information was stored on pieces of paper in filing cabinets. It's fairly easy to find one piece of information in a filing cabinet, but collecting together information to make lists is much more difficult and takes a long time. When we use a computer, the data stored takes up less space, and it is much easier to look things up. The computer can search the data it stores very quickly and can present the results of the searches in many different ways and print them out. This can make the information that has been stored much more useful.

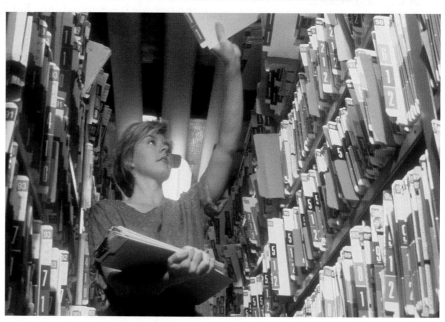

*Paper records in a health centre take up lots of space*

If health records in a hospital or health centre are stored on paper it's quite easy to find the record for one person. As you can see from the photograph there are lots of records, and to collect information on the age and sex of all the people suffering from one particular disease, for example, would mean that someone has to read the records of all the patients and copy out the information. This would require a great deal of effort and take a long time. If the health centre stored their records on a computer, a list of the information needed could be produced in only a few minutes. (You will find a detailed study of the information technology systems in a health centre in Chapter 15.)

# How does a computer store data?

A computer can store a certain amount of data in its memory, but to store large amounts of data it has to have a **backing store**, where the data will stay even if the machine is switched off. The backing store is usually some kind of **magnetic disc**, although **magnetic tape** (stored on large reels) and **optical discs** (like compact discs) are also used.

A **database** is a store of data that the computer can read and process in a variety of ways. Getting the data out of the database and then putting it in context is called **information retrieval**.

The data in a database is organised into **files**. These files are sometimes called **data tables**. Some databases have just one file, others have a number of files which can be linked together. A file is a collection of **records**, each of which contains data about one person or thing. The data in the records is separated into **fields**, each field holding just one item of data. Every field in a record has its own name, and to make things easier for the people using the database this name usually relates in some way to the field's contents.

You can see a summary of this information in Figure 2.1. As you can see, a database is not really very different from files in a filing cabinet – it's the way we can use the stored data which is different.

| Q |
| --- |

**What is a backing store?**

**Write down three types of backing store.**

**What do we mean by the term information retrieval?**

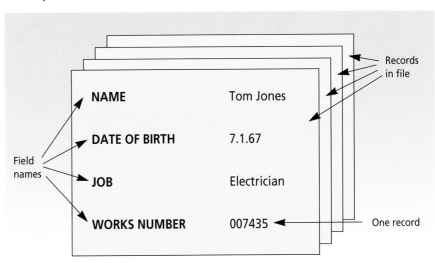

**Figure 2.1** *In this diagram you can see how fields, records and a file are organised in a database.*

# How do we get information out of a database?

To get information out of a database we have to **search** the file to find the records we need. (Some packages call a search a **query**.) We search by looking for a particular value in one of the fields. This value could be a word, a number, a date, a group of words or something else depending on what is in the field.

The database in Figure 2.2 is used by Ms Stillwell, who runs a small packaging supply business. Her customers order items and pay for them after they have been delivered. The file in this figure holds some details of the customer accounts – their names, customer number, and how much money they owe or have paid. You can see that these details are stored in separate fields. The fields have field names like SURNAME, CUSTOMER __ NUMBER and BALANCE.

| Customer number | Surname | Initials | Title | Balance | Area | Last order |
|---|---|---|---|---|---|---|
| 0001 | Smith | P. | Mr | -£233.56 | 04 | 27.04.1998 |
| 0002 | Ahmed | S. | Mrs | -£125.73 | 02 | 28.05.1998 |
| 0003 | Wells | P.J. | Ms | -£599.36 | 04 | 05.07.1998 |
| 0004 | Singh | V. | Mr | £2.65 | 01 | 19.05.1998 |
| 0005 | Lawrence | D. | Ms | -£45.50 | 03 | 10.03.1998 |
| 0006 | Bedford | L. | Mr | -£800.00 | 05 | 15.08.1998 |
| 0007 | Wilson | K. A. | Mrs | -£523.21 | 05 | 09.06.1998 |
| 0008 | Adams | H. T. | Mr | £56.20 | 01 | 29.05.1998 |
| 0009 | dhillon | K. S. | Mr | -£2.30 | 02 | 30.03.1998 |
| 0010 | Patel | V. N. | Mrs | -£264.21 | 02 | 29.06.1998 |
| 0011 | Braidwood | A. | Ms | £0.00 | 03 | 10.03.1998 |
| 0015 | Kramer | L. | Miss | £2.95 | 05 | 12.08.1998 |
| 0016 | Graham | J. | Mr | -£71.23 | 02 | 18.06.1998 |
| 0018 | Bates | T. | Mr | -£523.00 | 01 | 20.07.1998 |
| 0019 | Piejus | T. | Miss | -£350.00 | 05 | 30.07.1998 |
| 0020 | McFall | A. | Mr | -£605.85 | 03 | 19.08.1998 |
| 0021 | Penny | J.H. | Mr | -£695.20 | 03 | 14.08.1998 |
| 0023 | Smith | J. G. | Mrs | -£42.00 | 02 | 15.08.1998 |
| 0025 | Gallagher | I. D. | Miss | -£32.00 | 04 | 07.08.1998 |
| 0026 | Lee | M. | Mr | £56.00 | 04 | 23.07.1998 |

**Figure 2.2** *Part of the customer database used by Ms Stillwell.*

## SEARCHING FOR ONE RECORD IN A FILE

If Ms Stillwell wants to find a single record in her file – perhaps to check how much Mr Bedford owes – she could search for the value Bedford in the field SURNAME. The search she would set up would be:

SURNAME = Bedford

This works well because there is only one customer called Bedford, but it wouldn't work if she wanted to find information about Mrs Smith as

**Q**

**What is a primary key field?**

**Why are primary key fields important?**

there are two customers on her database called Smith. To be sure she gets just the record she wants she must search for a value which only that record has. She could find the record about Mrs Smith by searching for

CUSTOMER NUMBER = 23

because no other record has the value 23 in the field CUSTOMER NUMBER. Each record in this file has its own customer number, so by searching in this way she only extracts the one record she needs. A field that can be used in this way is called a **primary key field**.

## SEARCHING FOR A GROUP OF RECORDS

One of the most useful things about a computer database system is that it is easy to extract groups of records which all have certain things in common. With a conventional filing system we couldn't do this without going through every record. When Ms Stillwell wants to send reminders to customers who owe money she can search the file for

BALANCE < 0

In other words, she's looking for all the records that have a value of less than zero in the field **BALANCE**, which shows that the customer owes money. She can use the records found as a result of the search to print individual reminders to pay.

The general pattern for a search (or query) command that you would use to find a particular record or group of records is:

<name of field to look at> <type of comparison> <value to look for>

You can use these types of comparison:

- **Equal to (=)**
  To find all the records where the field contains the value to look for.
- **Less than (<)**
  To find all the records where the field contains a value lower than the value given. This works for letters and dates as well as numbers, so for example A is 'less than' B and 02/01/1998 is 'less than' 04/04/1999.
- **Greater than (>)**
  To find all the records where the field contains a value bigger than the value you have given. This works for letters, numbers and dates too, just like 'less than'.
- **Like (or sounds like)**
  To find words that sound similar. This is good for finding names which sound the same but are spelt differently.
- **Contains**
  To find words or phrases which have one part in common.

Some database packages use the symbols, others use words instead. Find out what comparisons your own database package can do and what symbols or words it uses.

## SEARCHES BASED ON MORE THAN ONE VALUE

The computer can carry out complex searches based on more than one value very quickly. All the conditions that have to be met (all the values involved) are linked together with the words **AND** and **OR**. If Ms Stillwell wanted to mail adverts to customers who live in a particular area and who haven't placed an order in 1998 she could use the search

### AREA = 4 AND LAST __ ORDER < 01.01.1998

This search would select all the records of customers in area 4 whose last order was before 1 January 1998. The records could be printed out so that these customers could be mailed. Some database programs store dates as numbers. When they do this the date has to be stored in the order.

### year, month, day

so that searches can be carried out easily. For this kind of database 1 February 1998 would be stored as 19980201 and any date before this would produce a lower number – for example, 3 January 1993 would be stored as 19930103.

# ■ *What the database produces*

The printout that you get from a database is called a **report**. You can produce a number of different reports from one database. A report can contain all the fields in each record, or just a few of them. It can be laid out so that it exactly suits the user's requirements. Some reports look like tables, with the field contents arranged in columns. In other reports the fields are spaced out over the whole sheet of paper. You can add headings and summaries of fields.

The report in Figure 2.3 includes five fields from Ms Stillwell's database file. The title (in this report 'Customers owing money') is a piece of fixed information which will be printed at the top of the report. The column headings have been added to the printout to show what each column contains but they are not quite the same as the field names – for instance 'Total owed' is a summary of the data in all of the records. The actual total is calculated by the computer. It adds all the **BALANCE** values for the selected records and puts the answer in the space reserved for it in the report. Most database programs can add up the values in the same field in each record and can do other calculations such as finding the average of all values.

## CUSTOMERS OWING MONEY

| Customer number | Surname | Initials | Title | Account Balance |
|---|---|---|---|---|
| 0001 | Smith | P. | Mr | -£233.56 |
| 0002 | Ahmed | S. | Mrs | -£125.73 |
| 0003 | Wells | P.J. | Ms | -£599.36 |
| 0005 | Lawrence | D. | Ms | -£45.50 |
| 0006 | Bedford | L. | Mr | -£800.00 |
| 0007 | Wilson | K. A. | Mrs | -£523.21 |
| 0009 | dhillon | K. S. | Mr | -£2.30 |
| 0010 | Patel | V. N. | Mrs | -£264.21 |
| 0016 | Graham | J. | Mr | -£71.23 |
| 0018 | Bates | T. | Mr | -£523.00 |
| 0019 | Piejus | T. | Miss | -£350.00 |
| 0020 | McFall | A. | Mr | -£605.85 |
| 0021 | Penny | J.H. | Mr | -£695.20 |
| 0023 | Smith | J. G. | Mrs | -£42.00 |
| 0025 | Gallagher | I. D. | Miss | -£32.00 |
| | | | Total owed | -£4,913,15 |

**Figure 2.3**

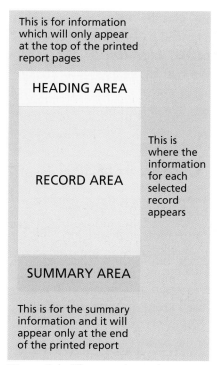

This is for information which will only appear at the top of the printed report pages

HEADING AREA

RECORD AREA

This is where the information for each selected record appears

SUMMARY AREA

This is for the summary information and it will appear only at the end of the printed report

**Figure 2.4** *The areas that make up a database report*

## SETTING UP A REPORT

A report like this has to be set up using the report designer in the database package before it can be used. Each database package does this differently, but most of them divide the report into at least three areas, as you can see in Figure 2.4.

Your database package might give you an extra area to put in the title of the report, and also for page summaries as well as the final report summary. When you set up the report any fixed information, like headings or explanations, is put into the places where it must appear. The fields that will appear for each record are **selected** and placed in the correct places in the **record area**. This only needs to be done for one record – the database package will work out how many records it can fit on a page when it prints the report and will set out each record in the same way.

When the layout for the report has been set up you can save it on disk as a report format with its own name. (The name you give it should tell you something about what the report is for.) The system might have limits on the length of the name, and might not allow spaces so you might have to call the monthly report 'Month' and the customer list just 'Customer'.

To get the printout shown in Figure 2.3, we need to do two things:

1 Select the records needed by searching for **BALANCE < 0**
2 Print the selected records using the correct report format.

Reports are not always lists. A report can be set up to print letters containing data from the records. For example, when customers don't pay

**Q**

What do we mean by a report?

Describe two different ways in which a report can be laid out.

Design a layout for a different report which might be useful to Ms Stillwell. What search command is needed for this report?

# REMINDER OF PAYMENT DUE

| | |
|---|---|
| Customer Number | 0001 |
| Name | Mr P Smith |
| Date of last order | 27.04.98 |
| Current balance of account | -£233.56 |

### Our terms are
*Payment within 28 days.*
*Payment is now outstanding*

## PAYMENT IS REQUESTED WITHIN SEVEN DAYS

**Figure 2.5** *The format used for a reminder slip, prepared from the database described in this chapter.*

their bills on time Ms Stillwell sends a reminder slip, in the format shown in Figure 2.5. She then prints them onto headed paper and sends them out to each customer who has owed money for more than 28 days.

When Ms Stillwell sets up this report format, all the fixed information and the field contents go into the record area so that everything is printed out for each record, and a page break is inserted at the bottom of the record so that each record is printed on a new sheet of paper.

The search used to select the records for this report is:

### BALANCE < 0 AND LAST __ ORDER < 01.08.1998

When she has selected the records, Ms Stillwell chooses the 'Reminder' report format – and the reminders are printed.

In a **relational database** the data is kept in more than one file. This is done to avoid having to store the same pieces of data over and over again. The files in the database can be linked. This means that you can include fields from different files in one report. A link can only be made if one field in each of the files matches. Ms Stillwell keeps information about suppliers and stock as well as customers. She needs to know where she buys her stock and how much she has but she doesn't want to have to type in the supplier name and address for every stock item she gets from that supplier. You can see how the data is divided into two files in Figure 2.6.

You can see some of the data stored in each of these files in Figure 2.7.

Using these two files we can produce an order like the one for Paper Products shown in Figure 2.8.

**Figure 2.6** *The structure of the stock and suppliers files showing how they can be linked using the supplier code fields in each file*

## Stock file

| Item_number | Item_name | Quantity | Supplier_code | Minimum level | Amount to order |
|---|---|---|---|---|---|
| 1055 | Carrier bag medium | 1500 | 002 | 1200 | 500 |
| 1057 | Carrier bag large | 900 | 002 | 1000 | 500 |
| 1059 | Poly bag small | 10500 | 001 | 10000 | 5000 |
| 1060 | Poly bag medium | 13500 | 001 | 10000 | 5000 |
| 1061 | Poly bag large | 12750 | 001 | 10000 | 5000 |
| 1062 | Paper bag small white | 18000 | 003 | 20000 | 5000 |
| 1063 | Paper bag medium white | 15600 | 003 | 20000 | 5000 |
| 1065 | Paper bag large brown | 12000 | 003 | 15000 | 5000 |
| 1066 | Paper bag medium striped | 12200 | 003 | 13000 | 5000 |

## Stock file

| supplier_code | Supplier_name | Supplier_address | Town | Post_code | Fax_number | Phone_number |
|---|---|---|---|---|---|---|
| 001 | The Carrier Co. | 126 Beech road | Bury | BY27 8LM | 0160 550441 | 0160 550372 |
| 002 | Plastic Supplies | 56–64 Range St. | Foxley | FX2 6YP | 0587 630493 | 0587 630821 |
| 003 | Paper Products | Unit 4 Iris Ind Est | Leeds | LD26 2KS | 0346 223654 | 0346 223547 |

**Figure 2.7** *The files contain details of stock suppliers. The stock file contains more than one record for each supplier.*

**Figure 2.8** *This order contains the Supplier-name, Supplier-address, Town and Post-code fields from the supplier file and the item name and amount-to-order fields from the stock file. Only records in the stock file which have the right supplier-code value are included in the order*

# Summary

- A database is a store of data which the computer can read. It can be accessed in many different ways.
- A file is a collection of related records.
- A record contains information about one person or thing. It is divided into fields.
- A field contains only one piece of data.
- Data is extracted by searching the database.
- Searches can be based on a unique value in one field to find a single record.
- Searches can find groups of records with a particular value in one field.
- More complex searches can be carried out by looking for specific values in more than one field.
- The output from a database is called a report.
- Lots of different reports can be produced from a single database.
- Records in different files (tables) in a database can be linked so that fields from both tables can be put in a report.

## SKILLS

When you have completed the work in this chapter you should be able to:

- Search an existing database to find one record.
- Search for groups of records with one or more things in common.
- Select and print out the report you want.

## Questions

**1** Explain what each of the following terms means:
File
Record
Field
Database

**2** Why is it important that the data we put into a database is accurate?

**3** A database program can do the following tasks:

Create or load a datafile.
Ask a single question.
Display results.
Save a file.
Describe three more tasks which the database program should be able to do. (MEG)

# Creating Your Own Database

When you create any kind of computer system, the process is divided up into these main stages:

- Identifying a need.
- Analysing what you must do to meet that need.
- Designing what you are going to produce.
- Implementing and testing your design.
- Evaluating how well your design meets the need.

The first step in creating your own database is to identify a need for a store of data which can be retrieved, perhaps in several different ways. The database you decide to set up yourself may be for use in one of the subjects you are studying at school or it may be concerned with an activity outside school. (You will find a list of suggested topics at the end of this chapter.)

A database is useful when:

- There is a large amount of information to be stored.
- The information fits into a regular pattern so each record can have the same structure.
- The database you set up will be used for more than one purpose or will be used more than once.

Once you have identified a need for a database you have to decide what the database must be able to produce. To do this you will need to think about the purpose of the database, the people who will use it and what they will want to know. When you have a clear idea of what you want your database to achieve you can begin the design work. Start by making a list of all the reports you need, with a description of what each one will contain. A very simple database system may only need one kind of report, but most will need two or more.

In the example in this chapter we will see how we can design and set up a database. Our database is to be used by the secretary of a fan club, who is the **end-user**. We must remember that we have to meet all the requirements of this end-user if our database system is to be a success.

# Stage 1: Identifying a need

The fan club we are working for has an expanding membership and the secretary is finding it difficult to keep in touch with everyone. A membership database will make the secretary's job much easier. Using a database is sensible because:

1 There are lots of members in the fan club (there is a lot of data).
2 We will have to store the same facts about each person so the data about each member will easily fit into the same pattern.
3 The secretary writes to the members regularly about different things so the data will be used many times and in different ways.

# Stage 2: Analysing what's needed

During this stage we look at what the club secretary wants the database system to do and identify the outputs we need.

1 The club has to send out material (such as newsletters) to all its members so the database must be able to produce name and address labels. These will have the member's name on one line and the address divided up into four lines, including the postcode.
2 Members sometimes forget to renew their subscriptions so the database must be able to produce letters to remind them that their subscription is due. These letters will need to be posted so name and address labels will be required as well.
3 Sometimes the club has special offers. The secretary thinks it might be useful to print a list of the members who have bought special offers in the past. This list should contain the member's number, name, address and a code number for the last offer purchased.

**Q**

Write down the main stages in the creation of any computer system.

It is important to know when a database would be useful. Describe three situations where you think a database would be useful.

# Stage 3: Designing what is to be produced

This stage is divided up into steps as there is quite a lot of designing to do.

## STEP 1: IDENTIFYING THE INPUTS NEEDED

We have to work out what has to be stored in the database to produce the outputs we need.

1 The club needs to store names and addresses. The address will need to be split up so that labels can be printed.
2 Each member should have a unique membership number so there is no chance of mixing up members with the same name. The date when the subscription was paid will have to be stored to produce the reminders.
3 The code number of the last offer purchased will have to be stored to produce the required list.

## STEP 2: CHOOSING THE RECORD STRUCTURE

We must now decide on the record structure. We have to work out how many fields we will have in each record and what should go into each field.

These fields have to be given names. Database packages don't always allow spaces in field names, so if we want to include a space we may have to put something in it. The best character to use is the underline character ( _ ). If we want a field called **LAST OFFER** we could call it **LAST_OFFER**. Often the length of a field name is limited as well, so we should give our fields fairly short names.

We have to decide how big each field needs to be to fit in all the characters needed (the **field length**). Fields can be of different types as well. A **field type** controls the kind of data which can be stored in the field.

● Character (or text) fields hold words and other characters (like @ or &).
● Numeric fields hold numbers, and you can usually fix the number of decimal places allowed. Some packages allow you to specify the **range** of numbers allowed.
● Date fields hold dates using two numbers for day, two numbers for month and either two or four numbers for year. If only two numbers are used for year then in the year 2000 the date will contain 00 for the year. If you store dates this way then 1 March 1998 will be 01/03/98 and 1 March 2000 will be 01/03/00. If you use date comparisons you won't get the results you expect. The computer will treat 01/03/00 as being before 01/03/98. For this reason you should always use four digits for the year part of the date. If you do this the dates would be 01/03/1998 and 01/03/2000 and comparisons will work properly.

| Field name | Length | Type |
|---|---|---|
| Membership_no | 5 | Numeric |
| Member_name | 25 | Alphanumeric |
| Address_1 | 30 | Alphanumeric |
| Address_2 | 30 | Alphanumeric |
| Address_3 | 30 | Alphanumeric |
| Postcode | 7 | Alphanumeric |
| Subscription_date | 8 | Date |
| Last_offer | 2 | Alphanumeric |

**Figure 3.1** *The record structure for a fan club's database.*

● Another field type is the logical or true/false field. This can hold a single letter or number to indicate whether the value in the record is true or false.

You can see the record structure we need for the fan club database file in Figure 3.1.

Not all database programs need you to specify the field length and field type when you set up the record structure. Some don't have a field type called 'date'. If this type isn't available in your database package you should store the date in a numeric field in the order Year, Month, Day. Storing the date in this order makes comparisons easy. The date 25 May 1998 would be stored as 19980525.

When you are deciding field lengths, think of the longest possible input for this field and use that length. For example, you will probably always need a longer field for the first line of the address than for the line containing the postcode.

## STEP 3: IDENTIFYING THE PROCESSING NEEDED

We must decide what searches the database program will have to do to select the correct records to produce the reports. This is the processing needed to get the reports the club secretary wants.

1 To produce the name and address labels no searching is needed – a label will be printed for each member. The order these labels are printed in doesn't matter so there is no need to get the database file into a particular order before printing.
2 For the subscription reminder notices the secretary needs to select those records with a **SUBSCRIPTION_DATE** of more than 1 year ago. The search to be used will be:

SUBSCRIPTION_DATE < TARGET DATE.

The target date is the earliest date when the subscription is still valid. For example:

SUBSCRIPTION_DATE < 01.06.1998

The records found are printed using the 'reminder notice' report format and then printed again using the 'label' report format to produce a set of address labels.
3 The special offers list must include the records which contain a number greater than zero in the **LAST_OFFER** field, meaning the member did buy something in the last special offer. The search to use will be:

LAST_OFFER > 0

The records found will be printed using the 'offer list' report.

**Q**

Describe the details needed to create a record structure.

Why should database programs without a 'date' field type store dates in the form YYYYMMDD?

**Figure 3.2** *The design for the label report for our fan club database. You can see that the address lines need to be longer than the one for the post code.*

**Figure 3.3** *The design for the offers report. This report needs the area for headings, which the label report didn't.*

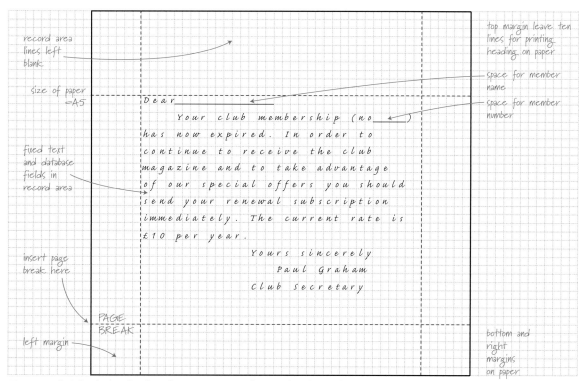

*Figure 3.4  The design for the subscription reminder, produced as a database report.*

The handwritten annotations read:

- record area lines left blank
- size of paper =A5
- fixed text and database fields in record area
- insert page break here
- left margin
- PAGE BREAK
- top margin leave ten lines for printing heading on paper
- space for member name
- space for member number
- bottom and right margins on paper

The letter text reads:

Dear _____

Your club membership (no_____) has now expired. In order to continue to receive the club magazine and to take advantage of our special offers you should send your renewal subscription immediately. The current rate is £10 per year.

Yours sincerely
Paul Graham
Club Secretary

## Q

**What do we mean by mail merging?**

**Personalised letters and junk mail are two examples of documents produced using mail merging. Collect some examples of personalised letters and junk mail, and decide which parts have been imported from a database.**

**What should you remember when you're creating a data collection sheet?**

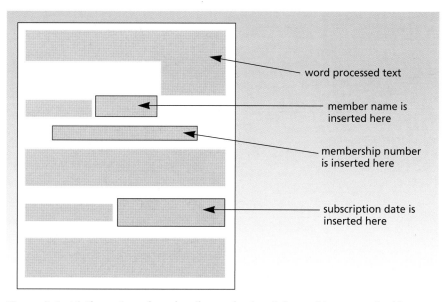

*Figure 3.5  Mail merging – how data from a database is inserted into a standard letter.*

Labels on figure:
- word processed text
- member name is inserted here
- membership number is inserted here
- subscription date is inserted here

## STEP 4: DESIGNING THE REPORTS

Each of the printouts needed has to be designed carefully so that it contains all the necessary information, the layout will be clear and everything will fit properly. Remember, you will often need to add headings or explanations, as well as the field contents, so the reader knows exactly what all the information means.

Always work out your design on squared paper first. This helps you fit everything in and gives you an idea of how the report will look. Take care to put each item in the correct area of the report. Our design for the label report is shown in Figure 3.2, and for the offers list in Figure 3.3.

We can set up the subscription reminder as a database report or we can type the reminder letter using a word processor and take the member's name and subscription date from the database record and put it into the correct place in the letter. This is called **mail merging**.

If we choose to use a database report we can design it on squared paper, with all of the text of the letter in the record area (you can see an example in Figure 3.4).

If we decide to produce the letters using mail merging then we will type the letter out using a word processor package capable of **importing** data from the database. We mark the places where data is to be put in and specify the file name and field names to be used. The way we do this will depend on the package used. The layout diagram in Figure 3.5 shows where data from the database will be inserted.

## STEP 5: DESIGNING THE DATA COLLECTION SHEET

A data collection sheet is a form that people fill in and which is used as the source of the data which goes into the database. For example, when a new member joins the fan club she will fill in all her details on a data collection form (this is sometimes called a data capture form).

When we design the form we must make sure that the person filling it in will write down the information they are supplying in the way we want it. We should always try to keep the order logical. People expect to give their name and address together when they fill in the form so we shouldn't ask for them to put their name at the top and their address somewhere at the bottom. If we expect a particular length of response then we should indicate on the form the number of spaces that are available, otherwise people will write things that don't fit into the database fields. The person filling in the form must be given very clear instructions so they're not left guessing about what they should write. Don't collect information you don't need. The design for the data collection form for the fan club is shown in Figure 3.6.

# Stage 4: Implementing and testing the design

This stage is also quite complex, so it has also been broken down into steps.

## STEP 1: SETTING UP THE DATABASE STRUCTURE AND THE REPORTS

With the database software package loaded into the computer, we create a new file for the fan club database. We name the fields in the record and enter any necessary information about field length and field type. It should then be saved to disk. When you want to enter data into your database you might find that the fields are displayed in the order you have put them in the record. Some database packages allow you to set up special input forms. Whichever method you use, you must make sure the data is entered in the same order as it appears on the data collection sheet. If your database package displays the field names in order for data entry, then the order of the fields in the record must be the same as the order the data is collected.

**Figure 3.6** *Design for the data collection form.*

Next we use the report design part of the database package to set up each report, working from the design sheets. We give these reports names or numbers and save them on disk.

We produce data collection sheets, using a suitable word processor package. (Chapter 4 covers word processing.)

## STEP 2: PUTTING DATA INTO THE DATABASE FOR TESTING

Now we enter some of the data so that we can test the database system. We don't have to put in all the data at this stage but we must enter enough for all the tests we need. We must be careful that the data we choose will test all the parts of the database system. At the very least we need:

● A record for a member who paid their subscription within the last year so we can check that we don't send reminders to people who have paid.

● A record for a member who didn't pay their subscription when it was due, so we can check that we do produce a reminder when one is needed.

● A record for a member who has bought a special offer, to check that this person appears on the offers list.

● A record for a member who has never bought a special offer, to check that this person does not appear on the offers list.

● It is a good idea to include an incomplete record as well, to see what happens if some of the field entries are missing.

We need to be very careful in working out the test data to be sure that all the searches will find records that contain the required data and leave out records which don't contain the required data.

You can see the data that must be entered for testing purposes in Figure 3.7.

| | | | | | |
|---|---|---|---|---|---|
| 00065 | Mr M. Evans | 14 Warwick Road Buxey Marway | M27 5BW | 12.11.1998 | 7 |
| 00052 | Ms L. Black | 83 Bailey Towers Bolton Road Rightmead | R56 1BD | 18.08.1998 | 0 |
| 00345 | Mr G. Singh | 28 High Street Foxley | F8 5TF | 05.06.1997 | 3 |
| 00012 | Ms A. Moru | 8 Coppel Place Shipdale | S18 6DD | 05.06.1997 | 5 |
| 00078 | Mr G Neville | 55 Barron Way Gawley | G15 4LB | | |

**Figure 3.7** *Data to be used for testing the database.*

## STEP 3: CARRYING OUT THE TESTS

**1 Testing printing of labels**
We select the labels report and give a print instruction. This should print out the address labels. The printout must be checked to make sure that it matches the design and that the data printed out is from the correct fields – it is also important to check that it fits the labels!

**2 Testing printing of subscription reminders**
To check that subscription reminder letters are produced properly we have to carry out a search (searches are often referred to as queries). Many packages have no way of saving a search or query, so you'd have to enter it each time you search. The search we need to use is

$$\text{SUBSCRIPTION\_DATE} < 01.01.1998$$

This will select the records for members whose subscriptions are overdue. We then choose the reminder report from the list of reports available and print out the letters. We must check the letters to make sure that the correct records have been selected. We must check the layout of the letter to make sure that the fields are appearing in the right places and that everything fits on the page. When the letters are done we print out the labels for these selected records.

**3 Testing printing of the last offers list**
To make sure the last offers list prints correctly we must do a different search. This time the search we need is

$$\text{LAST\_OFFER} > 0$$

This will select all the records where an offer number has been entered. To get the list printed out we choose the 'offer list' report from the list of available reports and give a print instruction. Again, we must check that the printed output is laid out as we expected and that the correct records and fields have been inserted.

## STEP 4: WRITING INSTRUCTIONS

The secretary of the fan club will need some instructions so that he can use the database. These instructions (often called the **user guide**) must be very clear and must cover all the things the user might reasonably expect to be able to do with the database. In this case we should explain how to print out each of the reports. We also need to explain how to add, edit and delete records so that he can keep the data up to date. User instructions should also explain how to make **backup copies** of the database, what to do if something goes wrong and how to get back data which has been lost by using the latest backup copy.

When we write these instructions we must be careful about the use of technical terms. The fan club secretary might not be very familiar with computers and databases so we need to explain words which might not be understood.

**Remember** – any database which contains personal information about living people has to be notified under the Data Protection Act. Our fan club database would have to be notified unless all the members had agreed to the data being stored on computer.

# Stage 5: Evaluating the database system

It is always important to look at what has been achieved. We need to be sure that the database we have set up is doing everything the fan club secretary wants. We can also look for ways to improve the database system.

## Summary

The stages involved in setting up your own database are:

- **Identify a need.** It doesn't make sense to set up a big database to carry out a single search. If there isn't very much data it is usually better to deal with it manually.
- **Analyse.** Work out what the database should be capable of producing.
- **Design.** Work out what will have to be stored to produce the required outputs. Decide what processing will be needed. Decide on the record structure. Design the reports and data capture sheets.
- **Implement.** Set up the database record structure and reports. Produce data collection forms.
- **Test.** Make sure the system works as it should.
- **Document.** Write instructions for the person using the database.
- **Evaluate.** Look at what has been done and check if the system meets the requirements. See if it could be improved.

# Suggested topics for database work

Here are a few ideas for databases you could set up yourself. They have been divided up into different subject areas.

## GEOGRAPHY

A database about the use of buildings in your area could produce reports on uses of buildings in particular streets and locations of all the buildings used for a particular purpose.

A database about local tourist attractions could provide lists of attractions of different types with information on opening hours and transport details.

## HISTORY

A database about local historical figures could be used to produce lists of people with certain achievements – for example a list of local people involved in the foundation of charities.

## SCIENCE

A database about animals and plants in the school grounds could be used to produce reports on animals in a particular habitat (such as a pond), animals of a particular type and animals and plants seen at a particular time of year.

A database about chemicals could provide reports on chemicals important in particular industries, chemicals which are harmful pollutants, and chemicals with particular properties.

## TECHNOLOGY/DESIGN AND TECHNOLOGY

A database about materials could be used to produce reports on materials with certain properties, materials within a specified price range or materials available in specified sizes.

## NON-SCHOOL RELATED DATABASES

If you don't want to work on a database related to a school subject then you could try one of these.

A *zoo database*, to produce reports on different animals, animals from different continents and animals in danger of extinction.

A *library database*, to produce reports on overdue books, books on various subjects and books which are on loan.

## SKILLS

After completing the work in this chapter you should be able to:

- Examine a task and decide if it makes sense to use a computer database to handle the information.
- For any particular task, decide what reports the database has to produce and what must be in these reports.
- Design record structures which let you store all the data you will need to create the reports.
- Produce detailed report designs.
- Work from these designs to set up a database.
- Design and produce data collection sheets.
- Select test data and test that a database system works correctly.
- Write good, clear user instructions.
- Evaluate a database system – decide if it meets the requirements of the end user and suggest how it could be improved.

## Questions

1  A geography database is to be used to produce several reports on tourist attractions. One will be used to list places with beaches, another will list places of historical interest. Each list will name three hotels in each town and two main attractions, and will give the name of the nearest airport.

   a  Identify the data items that will have to be stored to produce each report.
   b  Work out the fields you will need in each record in the database.
   c  Design the report layouts.

2  Why is data sometimes coded when it is entered into a computer?

3  How is data stored in a database easier to handle than information stored in a filing cabinet?

4  Describe, in order, the steps you would take to design and set up a database.

5  a  Give **two** reasons why a school would put all its pupil records onto a computer database.
   b  The technician makes a backup of the data every day.
      i   What is a backup?
      ii  Why is the backup made?                    (MEG)

6  A headteacher decides to create a database of all the computer hardware in the school. Describe the steps involved in creating the database.                    (MEG)

**7** A software company sends information to its customers by personalised letter. These letters are created using mail merging. (MEG)

**a** Describe the processes involved in mail merging.
**b** The company is considering using electronic mail to send information to its customers. Describe the process of sending and receiving electronic mail.

**8** Part of a pupil database is shown below.

| SURNAME | FORENAME | CLASS | DATE OF BIRTH | OPTION 1 | OPTION 2 |
|---------|----------|-------|---------------|----------|----------|
| Khan | Abda | 5K | 3–4–81 | Geography | German |
| Pearce | Helen | 5K | 4–5–81 | Geography | History |
| Pearce | John | 5K | 4–2–81 | History | French |
| Pine | Jane | 5K | 5–3–81 | German | German |
| Pike | Sarah | 5L | 12–6–81 | German | French |
| Price | James | 5L | 2–6–81 | Geography | History |
| Prince | Steven | 5G | 3–4–81 | History | French |
| Purdey | Jean | 5K | 2–5–81 | German | French |
| Singh | Chula | 5L | 5–2–81 | History | French |

A watch has been found on a geography field trip. The watch has the initials JP inscribed on it.

**a** Describe how the database can be searched to find the owner of the watch.
**b** Why does the database contain a date of birth field and not an age field? (MEG)

**9** A pupil database contains two data files. The structure of the two files is shown below.

| **Pupils** | **Subjects** |
|------------|--------------|
| Pupil number | Subject code |
| Surname | Subject name |
| Forename | |
| Date of Birth | |
| Address 1 | |
| Address 2 | |
| Address 3 | |
| Contact phone number | |
| Home phone number | |
| Subject code 1 | |
| Subject code 2 | |
| Subject code 3 | |
| Subject code 4 | |
| Form | |

a Why is it better to store data in two separate files, rather than keeping it all in one file?

b Why is Date of Birth stored rather than age?

c To find all the pupils in the same form a search can be carried out. In this database package searches take the form

<fieldname> <comparison> <value>

a search for **surname = "Robinson"** would find all pupils with the surname Robinson.

Write down the search you would carry out to find all the pupils in the Form called 7B.

d The Head Teacher wants to be able to send personalised letters to the pupils' parent or guardian.

What extra field would be needed to allow the letters to be produced?

e The pupil record contains four subject code fields. Each of these contains the code of an optional subject studies for GCSE. subjects can appear in any option group. The system can produce this report.

---

**Pupil Options Report**

**Pupil Name:** Paul Freeman
**Form:**        1OS
**Optional subjects studied:**
  1. History
  2. Geography
  3. Information Technology
  4. Spanish

---

i Explain how subject names were included in this report.

ii The system also produces subject lists like the one shown below:

---

**Subject:**  Spanish
**Form:**     1OS

    **Name:**
    Rachel Brown
    Graham Ellis
    Paul Freeman
    Sunita Patel
    Mary Williams

---

The subject code for Spanish is 12. Simple searches can be linked together using the logical operators AND, OR and NOT. Brackets are used to make sure the separate parts are handled in the correct order.

Write down the search needed to select the correct records from the pupil file for this report.                              (NEAB)

# Communicating Information –

## Word Processing

### ■*IT and communication*

Information technology (IT) has had a huge impact on the way information is provided. One of the most obvious uses of IT is in preparing written information using **word processors** and **desktop publishing** (**DTP**) packages, but we also use IT to prepare and communicate visual information (pictures and graphs), using art and **graphics** packages. Film makers use computer generated images and animation to make animated (cartoon) films and also in combination with film using real actors. The animated film *An American Tail* was made using computer generated images including moving background images and in *Who Framed Roger Rabbit?* many sequences were produced by combining animation, computer images and real people.

IT is also vital in producing music and sound effects. Using computers we can sample, store, retrieve, mix, edit and distort sounds in various

> **Q**
>
> **Write down three ways of using IT to communicate information.**
>
> **Try to find out what is meant by the technique of 'morphing' which is used in film production.**

*Computers can be used to generate background images for cartoon films such as* An American Tail.

*Human action can also be combined with computer animation to produce realistic effects as in* Who Framed Roger Rabbit?

*Computers are used in sound recording to mix different sounds.*

ways. The resulting sounds could not be produced by any conventional musical instruments (see Chapter 7 for more about sound).

**Multimedia** presentations use a combination of high resolution pictures, video sequences, sound and text to present information. Multimedia presentation requires huge amounts of stored data – **CD-ROM** is often used to store it instead of magnetic disks.

In the rest of this chapter we will look at word processing. You will find out more about graphics in Chapter 6 and about sound in Chapter 7.

# ■ *Word processing*

You are most likely to begin to use IT to communicate information using a word processor to produce a piece of written work – perhaps a review of a film you've seen.

## ADVANTAGES OF WORD PROCESSORS

Using a word processing package to prepare and print text has several advantages over using pen and paper or an old fashioned typewriter:

- Altering what you have typed (either to correct mistakes or to improve and rearrange your first draft) is easy.
- You can save your document on disk and reload it any time you need it.
- You can save standard layouts for documents, so if you want to produce lots of similar documents you can put them together more quickly than if you had to start from the beginning each time.
- Many word processor packages allow you to bring in (import) material from other packages (like pictures, charts and data from databases) so you can produce impressive reports easily and quickly.

# Using a word processor

The things you can do with a word processor will depend on the package you are using, but all packages will at least allow you to do the following:

- Insert text
- Delete text
- Justify text
- Move text around
- Alter the margins
- Alter the line spacing
- Use tabs
- Alter the way the text looks (for example by using underlining, italic, bold or changing the font).

When you begin to use a word processor or start to use a new word processing program it is a good idea to use an existing **text file** to find out how to carry out basic editing tasks. Most word processing packages have a few of these text files for you to experiment with and to practice your word processing skills. Once you are familiar with the operations your word processor offers you will be able to produce tidy, impressive documents in whatever style you choose.

Let's look at a few of these features in more detail.

**Rabbits**

Rabbits are small mammals. They live as wild animals but tame ones are often kept as pets. (Wild rabbits are a grey-brown colour.) Tame rabbits come in a variety of different colours. They can also be more than one colour. Some are white with black ears, paws and noses.

**Rabbits**

Rabbits are small mammals. They live as wild animals but tame ones are often kept as pets. Tame rabbits come in a variety of different colours. They can also be more than one colour. Some are white with black ears, paws and noses.

**Figure 4.1** *Deleting text. The sentence circled in the top sample of text has been deleted from the one at the bottom. Note that the rest of the paragraph has been rearranged to close up the gap.*

## DELETING TEXT

To **delete text** (or 'rub it out') you move the **cursor** (a line or block which shows where you are in the document) to the end of the text you want to delete and press the backspace or delete key to remove the unwanted material. When you delete something the package rearranges the remaining text to fill up the space, as it has done in Figure 4.1.

**Rabbits**

Rabbits are small mammals. They live as wild animals but tame ones are often kept as pets. Tame rabbits come in a variety of different colours. They can also be more than one colour. Some are white with black ears, paws and noses.

**Rabbits**

Rabbits are small mammals. They live as wild animals but tame ones are often kept as pets. Rabbits eat corn and cereals, hay and green foods such as grass, lettuce and cabbage. Tame rabbits come in a variety of different colours. They can also be more than one colour. Some are white with black ears, paws and noses.

**Figure 4.2** *Inserting text. An extra sentence (circled) has been inserted in the text at the bottom. The rest of the paragraph has automatically been rearranged to make room for the new material.*

## INSERTING TEXT

To **insert** or add text, move the cursor to the position where you want the new words to go. Make sure that your word processor will make room for the extra text, rather than typing over what is already there and then type in the extra text. The package moves the rest of the text to make a space for what you have typed in. Figure 4.2 shows how text has been reshuffled to fit in inserted text.

**Rabbits**

Rabbits are small mammals. They live as wild animals but tame ones are often kept as pets. Tame rabbits come in a variety of different colours. They can also be more than one colour. Some are white with black ears, paws and noses.

**Rabbits**

Rabbits are small mammals. They live as wild animals but tame ones are often kept as pets. Tame rabbits come in a variety of different colours. They can also be more than one colour. Some are white with black ears, paws and noses.

**Figure 4.3** *Changing the margins of a block of text. The margins in the top sample have been changed to give the sample at the bottom. All the text has been rearranged to fit the new margins.*

## CHANGING THE MARGINS

If you alter the **margins** of your document the package rearranges the text to fit it in (you can see this in Figure 4.3). In some older word processing packages you will have to alter each paragraph separately.

**Rabbits**

Rabbits are small mammals. They live as wild animals but tame ones are often kept as pets. Tame rabbits come in a variety of different colours. They can also be more than one colour. Some are white with black ears, paws and noses.

**(Rabbits)**

Rabbits are small mammals. They live as wild animals but tame ones are often kept as pets. Tame rabbits come in a variety of different colours. They can also be more than one colour. Some are white with black ears, paws and noses.

**Figure 4.4** *The heading in the sample at the bottom has been underlined to make it more noticeable.*

## UNDERLINING TEXT

**Underlining** is often used to distinguish headings (as in Figure 4.4) or to emphasise important words (other ways of doing this are to use *italic* or **bold** text). To underline text, turn on the underlining option at the start of the text to be underlined and turn it off at the end. If you have already typed the words you might need to move the cursor and put special markers at each end of the text you want underlined or you may have to highlight the text by moving the cursor across it then select the underline option.

## WORKING WITH BLOCKS OF TEXT

You can handle **blocks of text** all at once. Different packages use different methods of marking the block of text you want to do something with – you might have to move the cursor to the start and add a special 'start of block' marker then move the cursor to the end and add an 'end of block' marker. In other packages you can **select** the text by highlighting it using the mouse. Once you have marked the block you can move it, copy it or delete it. Figure 4.5 shows how a block of text has been moved.

**Rabbits**

Rabbits make good pets but they have to be handled carefully. A big rabbit can do a lot of damage if it kicks with its strong back feet. Rabbits eat corn and cereals, hay and green foods such as grass, lettuce and cabbage. They need clean water to drink and must be kept in a cage which is protected from the weather.This cage must be big enough to let them move around freely.

**Rabbits**

Rabbits eat corn and cereals, hay and green foods such as grass, lettuce and cabbage. They need clean water to drink and must be kept in a cage which is protected from the weather.This cage must be big enough to let them move around freely. Rabbits make good pets but they have to be handled carefully. A big rabbit can do a lot of damage if it kicks with with its strong back feet.

**Figure 4.5** *Moving blocks of text. The sentence circled in the text at the top has been moved to a new position.*

## ALTERING LINE SPACING

You can alter the space between lines of text. The spacing you can use is probably either **single spacing**, with the lines close together (this book is printed single spaced) or **double spacing**, with more space between each line of text (you can see an example in Figure 4.6). Some packages allow you to vary the **line spacing** more. You can set line spacing for the whole of your document when you begin or can alter it as you go along. Use the line space command where you want the change to happen.

**Figure 4.6** *Here is some text that is double spaced – the space between the lines is very large.*

**Rabbits**

Rabbits make good pets but they have to be handled carefully. A big

rabbit can do a lot of damage if it kicks with with its strong back feet.

Rabbits eat corn and cereals, hay and green foods such as grass,

lettuce and cabbage. They need clean water to drink and must be

kept in a cage which is protected from the weather.This cage must be

big enough to let them move around freely.

## JUSTIFYING TEXT

The **justification** of the text is the way it is arranged on each line. You can choose to have your text **fully justified**, which means that the spacing between the words is adjusted so that they fill the whole line and the right and left edges are both even (as in Figure 4.7).

> **Rabbits**
>
> Rabbits make good pets but they have to be handled carefully. A big rabbit can do a lot of damage if it kicks with with its strong back feet. Rabbits eat corn and cereals, hay and green foods such as grass, lettuce and cabbage. They need clean water to drink and must be kept in a cage which is protected from the weather.This cage must be big enough to let them move around freely.

**Figure 4.7** *This text has been set fully justified – both edges of the text are straight.*

You can also have text left or right justified. When you **left justify** your text the package arranges it so that it lines up along the left hand side of the page, and the right hand side is uneven. If you **right justify** your text it all lines up along the right hand side of the page, but the left side is uneven (examples in Figure 4.8).

> **Rabbits**
>
> Rabbits make good pets but they have to be handled carefully. A big rabbit can do a lot of damage if it kicks with with its strong back feet. Rabbits eat corn and cereals, hay and green foods such as grass, lettuce and cabbage. They need clean water to drink and must be kept in a cage which is protected from the weather.This cage must be big enough to let them move around freely.

**Figure 4.8** *A piece of text that has been set left justified. You can see that the left hand edge is even, but the right hand edge is jagged.*

You can also **centre** your text. The package will arrange what you type so that it is in a central position between the margins. You will find centred text useful for headings and titles and can see an example in Figure 4.9.

> **Rabbits**
>
> Rabbits make good pets but they have to be handled carefully. A big rabbit can do a lot of damage if it kicks with with its strong back feet. Rabbits eat corn and cereals, hay and green foods such as grass, lettuce and cabbage. They need clean water to drink and must be kept in a cage which is protected from the weather.This cage must be big enough to let them move around freely.

**Figure 4.9**  *The heading has been centred over the text in this example.*

## USING TABS

**Tabs** are a way of moving the text cursor in bigger steps than the space bar. They are very useful for typing tables as you can use them to make sure all your columns line up. Your package probably has some tab markers already set, but if these are not what you want you can set your own. You will need to find out how this is done on the package you are using.

## ADDING GRAPHICS

Many word processing packages allow graphics to be added to a document. They don't usually allow as much choice of position of the graphic as a Desk Top Publishing package but they can be useful for simple layouts. Using this feature we can add a picture of a rabbit to the text.

>  **Rabbits**
>
> Rabbits make good pets but they have to be handled carefully. A big rabbit can do a lot of damage if it kicks with with its strong back feet. Rabbits eat corn and cereals, hay and green foods such as grass, lettuce and cabbage. They need clean water to drink and must be kept in a cage which is protected from the weather.This cage must be big enough to let them move around freely.

**Figure 4.10**  *A picture of a rabbit has been added to the text.*

## USING TABLES

Some packages allow you to add tables to your document. These tables can have lines separating the different sections so the divisions are clearer than just using tabs. You may also be able to shade the table in different colours.

## OTHER FEATURES

Your word processor may have other features, including different fonts in different sizes, like those in Figure 4.11. Find out what extra features your package provides and learn how to use them.

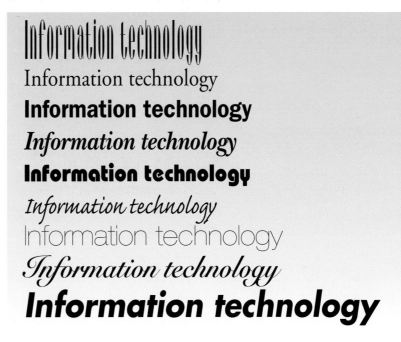

**Figure 4.11** *Some of the huge number of fonts you can use in word processing.*

## SAVING AND PRINTING

When you are sure you understand these editing commands and can carry them out, try **saving** and **printing** your work.

> **Be sensible** – always use your word processor's features sensibly – too many different fonts and sizes on one page will look untidy and disorganised and the impact of the page will be lost. When you are producing word processed text you should think about the people who will read it and what information you are trying to get across.

# Summary

- Information can be communicated in several different ways.

- When you use a word processor you can correct mistakes easily.

- A word processor lets you rearrange your work.

- You can save your work on disk and load it again later to make more copies or to edit your document.

### SKILLS

After completing the work in this chapter you should be able to:

- Produce a neat and tidy piece of work, using your word processing package to control the position of the text on the page.

- Save your work, reload it and print it.

- Use the editing facilities in your word processing package to alter and reorganise your work.

- Use different styles of text, underlining and different fonts to add impact to what you write.

# Questions

**1** In the table below, tick two items that are advantages that a word processor has over a typewriter.

The ribbon is changed automatically
It is quicker because the carriage returns automatically
It uses less paper
Work can be checked on screen before printing
The keyboard is smaller
The print is clearer                                        (MEG)

**2** Your Food Technology teacher has used a word processor to type out a recipe for a Victoria Sandwich cake.

> **1** Grease and line two sandwich tins. Heat the oven to 170° (mark 4).
>
> **2** Fold in the sifted flour and baking powder. Divide the mixture between the two tin and bake the cakes for about 25 minutes.
>
> **3** Cream together the margarine and sgar. Beat in the eggs one at a time.
>
> **4** Leave to cool and layer the cake with strawberry jam.

However, she has made two typing errors and has copied out the recipe in the wrong order. Explain how you could use IT to detect and correct the errors and the order of the paragraphs without retyping the whole recipe.        (MEG)

**3** A word-processing package has been used to create the documents shown below.

> The Paper and Bag Suppliers
> 67 High Street
> Manchester
> M99 8XX
>
> 15th June 1997
>
> Dear <TITLE> <SURNAME>,
>
> It has come to our attention that you have still not paid the bill for the goods we sent you in March of this year. Please pay within 7 days or we will have to take further action.
>
> Yours sincerely
>
> J. P. Williams
>
> Account Controller

---

*The Paper and Bag Suppliers*
*67 High Street*
*Manchester*
*M99 8XX*

15th June 1997

Dear <TITLE> <SURNAME>,

It has come to our attention that you have still not paid the bill for the goods we sent you in March of this year. Please pay within 7 days or we will have to take further action.

Yours sincerely

J. P. Williams

Account Controller

---

**a** Look at these two letters. List **three** features of the software that have been used to make the changes you can see. Explain how each feature has been used.   (NEAB)

**4** Middlebridge School displays the results of its annual sports day on a notice board. They use a word processor to produce this display, part of which is shown below:

---

Results

Year 7 Boys 100m

| 1st | P. Smith 13.82 s |
| 2nd | R. Finnegan 14.01 s |
| 3rd | S. Wilson 14.34 s |

---

**a** Put the following actions in the right order to show the stages in producing this display.
A. Print the display.
B. Type the words into the computer.
C. Check the screen for mistakes.
Write one letter in each box.

1st action      2nd action      3rd action

☐              ☐              ☐

**b** In order to improve the look of the display, the following changes were made:

| | Results | 1 |
|---|---|---|
| **Year 7 Boys 100m** | 2 | |
| 1st    P. Smith | 13.82 s | |
| 2nd    R. Finnegan | 14.01 s | |
| 3rd    S. Wilson | 14.34 s | 3 |

From the list below, choose the **three** ways in which the word processor has been used to make these changes. Enter these into the correct boxes marked 1, 2 and 3.

| | |
|---|---|
| Underlining | Centring |
| Double line spacing | Tabulation |
| Right justification | Full justification |
| Emboldening | Deleting                (NEAB) |

**5** Office staff now use computers for word processing.

**a** Text can be formatted when using a word processor. Give **two** examples of formatting.

**b** Give **two** advantages of using a word processor compared to using a manual typewriter.

**c** Give **two** ways in which office staff have been affected by the introduction of word processors.                (MEG)

# C H A P T E R

# Communicating information –

## Graphics

**G**raphics is a general term that is used to describe all the different kinds of pictures, drawings, charts and graphs that can be produced using a computer.

Graphics can be produced on a computer using **drawing packages**, **painting packages**, **computer aided design (CAD) packages** or **charting packages**. Some word processors allow you to produce graphics and many spreadsheets can be used to produce graphs and charts.

## *Choosing a graphics package*

**B**efore you choose a particular graphics package you must think about what you want to produce.

- If you need to produce accurate graphs and charts working from data you have collected then the graphics facilities of a spreadsheet package or a charting package will give the best results.
- If you need to illustrate a report or produce a poster then a drawing or a painting package will be best.
- CAD packages are good for accurately drawing to scale – for example when drawing designs for buildings or electronic circuits.

Let's look at the various packages in more detail.

## *Painting packages*

**U**sing a painting package you can 'paint' on the screen. Even simple packages let you do the following:

- Draw lines and shapes using the mouse.
- Use various ready-made shapes such as circles and rectangles.
- **Fill** in your shapes with different colours and patterns.
- 'Rub out' mistakes using the eraser tool.
- Spray colours on the screen using a spray tool.

- **Zoom** in on parts of the picture to alter small details.
- Print your picture out.
- Save your picture on disk so you can reuse it or change it later.

The picture in Figure 5.1 was made using a painting package. The first parts drawn were the sky and the sea. These are rectangles filled with colour. Everything else was drawn on top of this background. The birds started as lines and were altered slightly by zooming in on them and changing the colour of a few spots (each spot on the screen is called a **pixel**). The clouds were built up by spraying white and grey onto the sky. The cliff was painted using the mouse, in green and brown. It was then tidied up and the white foam was added by zooming in and altering the colour of some of the pixels. The boat was painted and tidied up in the same way.

Painting packages are usually very easy to learn to use but don't have as many facilities as drawing packages. The pictures are saved on disk by storing data about the colour of each spot on the screen. You can't usually change the size of parts of the picture and if you try to alter the size of the whole picture you could be disappointed with the result.

**Figure 5.1** *A graphic drawn using a painting package.*

# Drawing packages

Drawing programs have lots of different tools to make it easy to produce pictures. Using a drawing package you can:

- use straight lines or draw freehand lines as needed
- use ready-made shapes, such as circles and rectangles, which you can place anywhere in your drawing. You can adjust the size of these shapes at any time
- draw shapes and lines in different colours, and use different colours and patterns for filling different parts of the drawing.

*A selection of popular drawing packages, some of which have been used to produce artwork in this book.*

You can choose the tools and colours by pointing the cursor at icons (an **icon** is a little symbol or patch of colour) positioned around the edges of the screen. You can also choose some tools from menus which appear when you point at their names.

A picture produced by a drawing package is not stored in the same way as one produced by a painting package. Most drawing packages treat each shape you draw as a separate **object** and store its particular characteristics separately. You can alter the size of these objects easily and move them around on the screen.

**Figure 5.2** *This drawing was produced by combining the ready-made shapes available in a drawing package with freehand lines.*

The picture in Figure 5.2 has been drawn using some of the ready-made shapes available in a drawing package and some freehand drawing. You can make a drawing like this using a pointing device such as a **mouse**. It takes practice to be able to use a mouse quickly and accurately but you can remove any mistakes using the eraser tool. Once you have finished your drawing you can save it on disk so that you can use it again later. You can also print it out on a suitable printer. If you print a colour picture on a printer which can only produce black and white images, the picture will come out with a different pattern for each colour in the drawing. If you use a colour printer you should get a fairly good colour match between the picture on the screen and the printed picture (they probably won't look exactly the same because the colours are produced in different ways on the screen and on the paper).

## MAKING A DRAWING

When you make a drawing on your computer, you will probably want to use a mixture of ready-made shapes and freehand drawing.

### Copying objects
If you want to repeat a shape in the drawing, you only need to draw it once – then you can make extra copies of it using your package's copy or **duplicate** facility (most drawing packages have this). You can then move the copies wherever you want them on the screen.

### Changing the size of objects
Your drawing package will almost certainly let you change the size of the objects in your drawing. If your package lets you do this you might find it easiest to draw the shapes quite big and then shrink them to the size you want them to be. Most packages have a magnify or zoom facility to allow you to draw fine details accurately.

### Overlapping objects
Getting different parts of your drawing to overlap properly requires some thought and planning. If the package is fairly simple you might have to build up your drawing starting from the background and adding the objects towards the front of the picture.

### Flipping and rotating objects
Your drawing package will let you rotate an object or flip it over to produce a mirror image. In simple packages you may only be able to rotate in steps of 90° at a time but more advanced packages let you rotate objects by any amount you want.

**Figure 5.3** *A basic shape can be copied, flipped and rotated.*

### Stretching and distorting objects

Special effects can be produced by stretching an object so that its shape changes. This is usually easy to do. Just select the object and pull in the direction you want it to stretch. You can only stretch whole objects or groups of objects, not just part of an object.

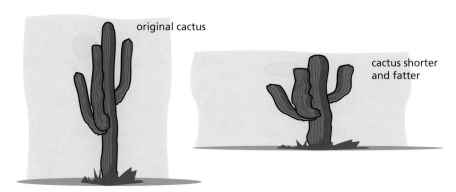

original cactus

cactus shorter and fatter

**Figure 5.4** *Objects can be stretched and shrunk to change their shapes. The cactus drawing has been stretched sideways and shortened from top to bottom.*

### Correcting mistakes

Whatever you are drawing, you are bound to make some mistakes! You can usually remove the last mistake you've made using the 'undo' command, provided you do this straight away but if you've drawn something else since you made the mistake, 'undo' probably won't work. You can use the 'erase' tool to rub out the part that's wrong, but this will leave a hole in the background and you'll have to redraw that part. The most sensible way to get round this problem is to save your work frequently. If you do this, and you make a big mistake, you can always go back to the last correct drawing you saved on the disk, which means you won't have to redraw the whole picture.

### Layers

More advanced drawing packages allow you to work on different **layers** in a picture. You can draw each layer separately then put them together to produce the final drawing. In packages like this the various parts of the drawing are objects.

### Grouping objects

In the drawing of the caterpillar and toadstools (Figure 5.2), each segment of the caterpillar body, the stalks and knobs of its feelers, each eye and its mouth are all separate objects. These objects were put into a single **group** once the caterpillar had been assembled. Grouping allows the whole caterpillar to be moved around and resized as if it was one object.

**Figure 5.5** *A more complicated drawing prepared using the copy and graded filling features available in a drawing package to give a three-dimensional effect.*

When we drew Figure 5.2, we kept the completed caterpillar in the front layer of the picture. The two toadstools were drawn freehand, the objects that made them up were grouped and then placed in the back layer of the picture so the caterpillar could be positioned in front of one of them.

We have used some of the features just described to draw the bunch of grapes in Figure 5.5. We drew one grape and one leaf then made more of them using copy, and arranged them so they overlapped. Some of the leaves had to be rotated first, then dragged into place using the mouse. We altered some of the colours to make the front leaves look paler than the back ones. Colouring a shape is called filling it. We also **graded** the fills to help the grapes look rounder. This works because each fill starts from a small pale area and becomes darker towards the edges of the shape.

## Questions

1 What is a 'graphic'?
Write down the name of a drawing and painting package that you use in school.

Make a list of the ready-made shapes that are available in your package.

Make a list of the other tools and facilities which are available with this package.

2 Use newspapers and magazines to cut out and collect different examples of company logos. For each logo try to answer the following questions.

Are colours used? If so, how many are used?
Does it contain a picture or just text?
Is there a connection between the logo and what the company does?
Is it a simple or a complicated design?
Is it a design which will be easily recognised?
Do you think it's a successful logo?
What are the features which make a successful logo design?

3 Use a drawing and painting package, plus what you have found out about successful logos, to design a logo for your school.

# Using computer aided design (CAD) packages

CAD packages are designed to make it easier to produce detailed plans and accurate technical drawings. Your package will probably have the following features:

- sets of ready-made symbols for standard types of drawings – such as electrical circuits
- standard ready-made shapes as tools for you to use
- it will allow you to use different types of line for drawing
- it can automatically round the corners of shapes
- it will let you fill shapes with ready-made shading patterns or patterns you have designed yourself.

A CAD package can also be used to carry out calculations. It can calculate the actual length of lines from a scale, and work out the actual areas of shapes which have been drawn to scale. The drawing in Figure 5.6 was produced using a CAD package.

Once a design has been produced using a design package it is often possible to produce a program to control the production of an object by a machine. This is called Computer Aided Manufacture (CAM).

CAD packages are designed for detailed work and it is important that the screen **resolution** of your computer system is good enough to show this detail. Resolution is the number of separate points, across and down, which can be displayed. Output to the printer or plotter is also detailed and very accurate and some printers can't achieve this degree of accuracy. You should check what your printer or plotter can do before starting on a detailed drawing.

---

**Q**

**What do the initials CAD stand for?**

**What type of drawings are best carried out using a CAD package?**

**What are the features of a CAD package which make it suitable for these types of drawings?**

---

Stephen Ramkaran
Group 3B
CAD application
November 1999

**Figure 5.6** *The sort of graphic you can draw using a CAD package.*

# *Choosing the right package*

When you are doing graphics work it is important that you select a suitable package for the task you have to carry out.

- If you want colour, shading and lots of fills then choose an art or painting or drawing package.
- If you want detailed and accurate line drawings then choose a CAD package.

## Summary

- Graphics packages are designed to be used for drawing. They are not usually very good at handling lots of text.
- Graphics packages have ready-made shapes (called tools) which you can use to help make the drawing you need.
- Freehand drawing with a mouse is not easy! Save your work regularly so if you do make a mistake you can go back to the last correct version.
- In a drawing package, once you have drawn an object you can make extra copies of it and rotate them or move them around on the screen. This can make it a lot easier to produce a detailed drawing.
- CAD packages are intended for producing plans and technical drawings. Using a CAD package you can produce very accurate and detailed drawings.
- A CAD package provides tools and features not found in ordinary graphics packages.
- CAD packages can be used to calculate lengths and areas. They can also measure angles.
- To get the best out of a CAD package takes time and requires a high resolution screen and printer.

### SKILLS

When you have completed the work in this chapter you should be able to:

- Choose the appropriate type of graphics package for a particular task.
- Produce pictures using each type of package.
- Save your pictures and reload them for further work.
- Use the tools in your package to make drawing tasks as easy as possible.
- Using your drawing package, or your CAD package, make sensible use of layers and grouping of objects to build up drawings.

## Questions

1 A school has recently bought a new graphics package. The package has **tools** that carry out various tasks. Five of the different **tools** that are available in the graphics package are given below. Explain clearly the purpose of each.

a Freehand drawing
b Pre-defined shapes
c Text
d Copy
e Palette                                                    (NEAB)

2 Describe how Information Technology can be used to design the layout of a computer room.                    (MEG)

3 Ring **two** reasons for using a graphics package on a computer.

Colour can be changed easily.
Parts of a design can be copied quickly.
It does your homework for you.
It will store pupil records.
You can control a floor turtle.
To do the school accounts.                                (MEG)

# CHAPTER

# Communicating Information –

## Desktop publishing

### ■ *What can DTP do?*

Using desktop publishing (DTP) software you can design page layouts and combine text and graphics in almost any way you choose. You can also very easily rearrange parts of a page to try out different ideas. Some packages work only in black and white but most allow you to use colour. Your DTP package will provide at least these features:

- a good range of fonts in a variety of sizes
- basic text entry and editing facilities
- some drawing facilities
- it will allow you to import text from a variety of word processing programs
- you should also be able to import files produced by various painting and drawing packages or files created by scanning images using a **scanner** like the one in the photograph
- you will probably find that the package also has a collection of pictures in various sizes ready for you to use. These pictures are called **clip-art** and can be put onto your page wherever you want them. You can see some examples of clip-art in Figure 6.1.

**What does 'importing' mean when we are talking about DTP packages?**

**What is a font? Find out the names of some different fonts and note the ones that the DTP package in your school has.**

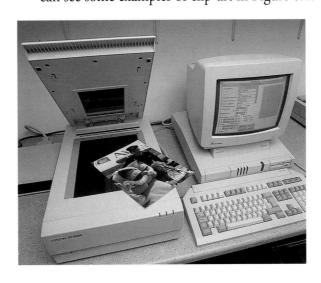

*A scanner for scanning images onto a computer screen.*

**Figure 6.1** *Some examples of clip-art.*

# ■ *Getting started*

Before you set up your page you will need to do some design work. You will need to make the following decisions:

- What information do you want to get across? (Is it a story, a set of instructions, a news article?)
- Who do you expect to read the finished page? (Friends or strangers? Experts or beginners? Children or adults?)
- Where and how will the page be read? (In class with a teacher? On a bus journey to work? At home in leisure time?)

All of these will influence the way you design your page. You will find it helps to make a few notes about these things early on so that later you can check that the pages you produce do what you set out to achieve.

# Planning the page
## STEP 1: DECIDING ON THE BASIC PLAN

You will need to make some decisions about how the page is going to be laid out. Figure 6.2 shows some possible layouts you could use.

**Figure 6.2** *Examples of layouts possible in portrait orientation.*

If you are producing a newsletter then you will probably choose a layout with several columns, partly because this layout is traditional for newsletters, but mainly because narrow columns are easy to skim through to find topics of interest. You must be realistic and remember that people will probably not read everything in your newsletter.

If you are presenting advertising material it must make a quick impact. A poster or leaflet must put its message across at the first glance if it is going to be successful. You will need to use large fonts and illustrations on a poster, so a column layout wouldn't work very well. Remember, people will probably not spend long reading what you produce. Keep it fairly simple and short.

The next figure shows some examples of advertising material. Some of them are very effective but others are not so good. Try to work out the good and bad features of each of them.

**Figure 6.3** *Good (and not so good) examples of advertising material.*

Sometimes we need to make a quick impact at first sight, but also need to provide quite a lot of detailed information – for example, in a publicity leaflet for a theme park. In addition to this, the number of pages we can use might be limited because of the cost. A great deal can be achieved using just one sheet of paper. If we turn the page sideways (this is called **landscape** orientation – this page is printed in **portrait** orientation) then divide it into columns, we can produce a page which folds into three sections. The column that forms the 'front cover' of this leaflet can be used to make immediate impact and the inside columns and back cover can contain more detailed information. You can see how this works in Figure 6.4.

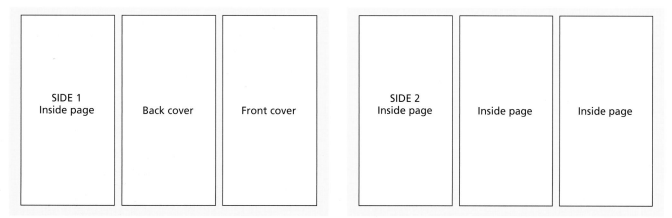

**Figure 6.4** *The way columns are laid out to produce a folded leaflet.*

If you use this kind of layout for a leaflet then you will need to be very careful in deciding what information to put in each column to make the best impression, but the result can be worth the extra effort. You can fold paper in other ways as well – some are shown in Figure 6.5. Use some sheets of paper to try to work out other ways of folding it.

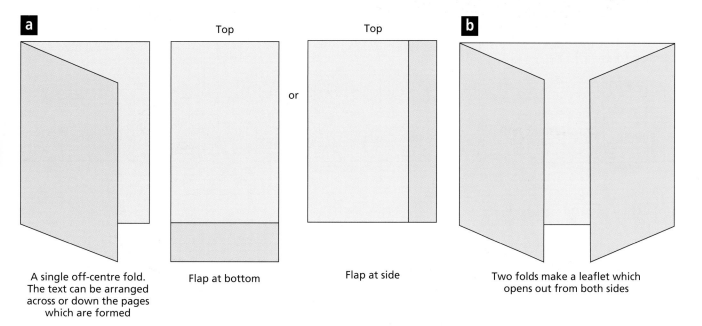

**Figure 6.5** *Ways of folding one sheet of paper.*

If your finished publication is going to be several pages long then it's a good idea to try, as far as you can, to keep the same style of layout all the way through, otherwise the overall effect can be very confusing and off-putting. If you do need to change the style of layout, keep the changes to a minimum.

## STEP 2: ADDING TEXT AND GRAPHICS

Once you have completed your basic plan, it is time to work out where the text and illustrations will go and what information each item will communicate. Remember, the **white space** (empty space with nothing printed on it) of a page is just as important as the written material and pictures in creating impact. You don't have to fill every bit of the page – leave gaps between blocks of text and around pictures so that they will show up better.

Before you start to set up the page on the computer you should draw some plans to show what it will look like. Start with small plans (like those in Figure 6.6) and draw in the areas you intend to fill with text and pictures. You don't need to write in the words, just use shading or lines.

**Figure 6.6** *Possible designs for the newsletter.*

**Figure 6.7** *The rough design for the newsletter.*

If you intend to use colour in the final product then put this on your plan so you can see the impact. Try several ideas then produce a full-size plan (you can see one in Figure 6.7) and look at it to evaluate the effect of the layout itself, without any information in it.

In the design sheet in Figure 6.7, black lines have been used to indicate text, and shading to indicate pictures. Large fonts are shown by thick black blocks. Don't be tempted to write in the words – at this stage you need to look at the layout on its own.

## STEP 3: PREPARING THE TEXT

There are two approaches to the task of preparing the text. Whichever method you use, when you prepare your text, keep your readers in mind. Think about the words you are using and the message they are putting across. Don't pad things out just to fill up space.

**Q**

Look at a typical page from your favourite magazine. Describe the layout of this page – the size and number of the columns, the size of the text. Draw a diagram (similar to the style of Figure 6.6) to show this layout.

What proportion of the page is taken up by:

small text (body text)?
graphics?
headings?
white space?

How does the page design draw the reader's attention to various items?

Repeat the exercise using a magazine aimed at a different market.

Compare the two layouts you have looked at. How is each layout appropriate for the readers that magazine is aimed at?

*The company logo of Hodder Headline plc.*

*Importing text from a word processor*

You can use a suitable word processing package to type in and edit the text, save the text on disk, and then import it into the page in your DTP package. This is usually the easiest option if there is a lot of text because editing is usually much easier in the word processing package than in the DTP software.

If you use a word processor, try to avoid using anything that is not straightforward text. Don't alter the margins or use special fonts or styles. Use left justification so that the spaces between the words will all be the same size. You can adjust these things later in the DTP package – if you do them in the word processor then you might have problems importing the file into the DTP package.

At this stage you must check that you have saved the text file in a way that is acceptable to the DTP package you are using. Different packages save text in different ways, called **file formats**. You will need to find out what file formats the DTP package accepts and which ones your word processor can produce when you save work on disk. The three letters after the full stop in the file name may need to match. If you save your text file in a format the DTP package can't use then it will either not import it at all, or it will be imported but won't make sense. Choose a format that both packages can use and always save your text files in this format.

You will find it easiest to work with your text if you separate it into sensible sections – if your finished page is going to have two completely separate blocks of text then save each block of text in a separate file. Use a sensible naming system for your files as you can end up using several files and you might not always remember what is in them!

*Working directly in the DTP package*

The second approach to preparing text for DTP is to type it directly onto the page using the DTP software. This works well for headings and short sections of text but most DTP packages are not designed for editing lots of text and it can be a problem. If you intend to use this method then you should work out what the text will be and where it is to go before you start to type so you don't have to change or edit it very much.

## PREPARING GRAPHICS

We use graphics on a page for several reasons – but remember, don't use graphics just to fill leftover space!

- Graphics – graphs, maps and diagrams – can often give information much more clearly than a description in words.

- Describing something realistically is sometimes hard to do in words – photographs do this very well.

- You can often appeal to people's feelings more effectively using a careful selection of graphics than by using words – again, photographs usually work best.

**Q**

**Look at the examples of the use of graphics in this chapter and try to work out why each graphic has been included. Could any have been left out?**

**Write down the name of the DTP package you use in school.**

**Which file formats will this package accept when importing text?**

**Which file formats will this package accept when importing graphics?**

**Give four reasons why you might use graphics on a page.**

**How would you include photographs in a document prepared using DTP?**

- Including graphics can break up your page and make the whole document much more interesting to the reader.

- A graphic can become associated with a particular company. The company can then use it to promote their image and their products. This kind of graphic is often called a logo.

*Preparing your graphic*

Once you have decided why you want to include a graphic, you need to prepare it. If it is a line drawing you could draw it using a suitable graphics package, as we saw in Chapter 5, and produce a file ready for importing into the DTP package. As with text, you need to be careful to save your graphic in a file format that your DTP package can use. If you find it hard to produce a reasonable drawing like this you could use clip-art.

You can also **scan** a picture and produce a file ready to import onto the page that way. A scanner measures the light reflected from a picture working from one edge to the other. The scanner software uses these measurements to produce an image on the screen and you can save this in a file on disk. If you choose to scan a drawing you will almost certainly need to tidy up the scanned image before you can use it. The scanner software will let you do this but it can take a very long time.

If you want to include photographs you will have to use a scanner to produce the necessary files. Photographs can be difficult to scan successfully. You might need to try a few times, varying the scanner settings, before you are satisfied with the result. Occasionally you get a better result if you photocopy the original photograph and then scan the copy.

## STEP 4: PUTTING THE PAGE TOGETHER

You then use your DTP package to put all the elements together. A DTP package can be either page-based or document-based.

A **document-based package** is good for working on several pages, all with the same basic layout. You can set up the layout as a master page then add extra pages, with the same basic layout, as you need them. This type of package lets imported text which won't all fit on one page flow onto the next page, so you don't have to worry about the length of text files.

A **page-based package** is more flexible if you need to change the layout from one page to the next, but if the text is too long for the space available it won't automatically be continued on the next page.

*Preparing a page template*

Most DTP packages need you to set up columns and boxes (called **frames**) for the text and graphics to go into before you can put anything else on the page. It is very easy to move the frames and their contents around on the page or to change their size to make everything fit properly. Find out about the package you will be using and try setting up your own page plan – the **page template**.

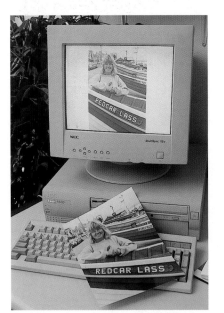

*Pictures can be converted to images on a computer screen.*

**Figure 6.8** *The page template used for the newsletter showing frames. These will be the same in every issue.*

When you have set up all the boxes your page template will probably look something like the one in Figure 6.8. You are now ready to put your text and graphics into the page.

### Putting in the text

To add text from a text file select the first frame to be filled and choose the font you want to use if necessary. Give the command to import a text file (this is sometimes called a **story**). Enter the name of the text file you want to use – and if everything goes right the text will be loaded. It might appear straight away in the selected box or you may need to use another command to insert the text on the page, depending on the package you're using. You can now alter the font and size of the text as you want. Most DTP packages allow you to link frames so that a piece of text which is too long to fit in the selected frame flows into the next one, even if it is on a different page.

### Special text effects

DTP packages will provide a range of special effects for text. These can be used to make headings stand out. Here are some examples.

**Figure 6.9** *Some of the different text effects we could use for the title*

**Figure 6.10** *Some of the text has been inserted into one frame of the template*

You will probably want to type some of the text straight onto the page. In most packages, to do this you select the box, position, and the font you want and start typing. Some packages use a separate **text editor** (like a simple word processor) and then you must give an 'edit text' command before you can do anything to your text. In this sort of package you will put the text onto the page using another command. In Figure 6.10 some text has been put into the basic page template we saw in Figure 6.8.

### Putting in graphics

Putting your graphics on the page is very like putting in text. Select the box, give the 'load picture' command, enter the file name of your graphic and your picture should load straight into the page. Be patient – this could take some time if the picture is large. You may need to adjust the size of the frame if it's not the same shape as the picture. If you find the picture is long and thin, shorten or widen the frame until it looks right, if it's short and fat, lengthen the frame or make it narrower. You can stretch pictures deliberately to create a special effect. Figure 6.11 shows the page we saw earlier with a graphic in place. The final page, with all the text and graphics in place is shown in Figure 6.12.

**Figure 6.11** *The newsletter first page, with a graphic imported into one of the frames as well as some text.*

**Figure 6.12** *The final page, with all the text and graphics in place.*

**Figure 6.13** *You can produce special effects using DTP packages – here are a few.*

**Q**

Write down the stages you go through as you create a document in DTP.

For the DTP package which you use in school, write down the commands you need or the method you use to:

- create a frame
- resize a frame
- move a frame
- delete a frame
- enter text straight into a frame
- import text
- import a graphic
- alter the font style of a section of text
- alter the font size of a section of text
- resize a graphic
- save a document
- print a document.

## Special effects

If you want text to flow around a graphic then you must make sure that you put the graphic on the page before the text. To find out how to do this and how to produce other special effects, you will need to read the instructions supplied with your DTP package. You should be able to add borders with shadows to frames and also overlap frames if you want. The page in Figure 6.12 shows some of the special effects you can get using DTP.

*The finished product. All of these leaflets were produced using DTP packages.*

## STEP 5: PRINTING THE PAGE

When you have completed your page *and you have saved it on disk*, you are ready to print it out. You must *always* **save** your work before trying to **print** it – if anything is going to go wrong, printing is the stage when it is most likely to happen and if you haven't saved your page you could lose all your hard work!

The quality of the output you get will depend on the type of printer you are using. Laser and inkjet printers will produce very good output. Your package will probably be able to send output to several different types of printer. You might need to select the right kind before giving the print command. The way you do this will depend on the package you are using so you will have to find out.

# Summary

- A DTP package lets you lay out pages in any way you want.
- It provides a range of fonts in a variety of sizes.
- Graphics can be put anywhere on the page.
- You should design the page before putting it together.
- The text and graphics can be prepared using other packages then imported into the page.
- Clip-art is available with many DTP packages and can be used as ready-made illustrations.
- Various special effects can be produced.

# *Suggestions for DTP work*

- Produce an advertisement for a school play, concert or sporting event.
- Produce a class newspaper.
- Produce a leaflet giving information about one of your hobbies to encourage others to try it.
- Produce a sheet to tell strangers how to get to your school from outside your town.
- Produce fact sheets about how to stay healthy. You could concentrate on healthy eating, exercise or the dangers of smoking.

## SKILLS

When you have completed the work in this chapter you should be able to:

- Design layouts for pages for particular purposes.
- Select suitable graphics for the page.
- Set up the page template using the DTP software.
- Import text and graphics and arrange them on the page.
- Save, retrieve and print pages.

## Questions

1 A man has decided to sell all his golfing equipment. He plans to advertise all of the items he has for sale. He will put copies of his advert in the local shops and in the golf club. Below is a copy of the advert he has produced using a DTP (Desk Top Publishing) package.

---

**FOR SALE – GOLF EQUIPMENT**

For sale FULL set of golf clubs, 10 irons, 4 woods and a putter.
All clubs are in excellent condition and carry a well known brand name.
Also for sale golf trolley, umbrella, golf shoes (size 9) and 100 golf balls. £150 for a quick sale.
*Telephone Dave Brown on 565656.*

---

Describe **five different features** of a DTP (Desk Top Publishing) package that he could use to improve the advert. Give a reason why each **feature** might be used.          (NEAB)

2 A Desk-Top Publishing package will be used to produce an 'Anti-Smoking' leaflet aimed at teenagers.
Name **four** factors that you would have to take into account when creating this leaflet. For each, give a feature of the Desk-Top Publishing package you would use to put this factor into practice. For example:
**Factor** – There should be no spelling mistakes in the leaflet.
**Feature of package** – The spell checker can be used.     (NEAB)

**3** A school has decided to have an open day for parents of children who may wish to come to the school in future years. It has been decided to use a Desk Top Publishing (DTP) package to produce a leaflet about the school for parents. A drawing of the planned leaflet is shown below:

  **i** The Desk Top Publishing package allows text and illustrations to be combined.

  Give three other ways in which using the package could improve the quality of presentation of the leaflet compared to using a manual typewriter.

  **ii** The Desk Top Publishing package allows text and illustrations to be moved around the page.

  Give three other ways in which using the package could give you control over the final design of the layout of the leaflet. (NEAB)

**4** You are producing a school magazine using a desktop publishing package. Compare alternative methods used to obtain pictures for inclusion in the magazine. (MEG)

# Communicating Information –

## Sound

Computers can be made to generate and recognise different sounds, using **peripheral devices** such as loudspeakers and microphones connected to the computer and controlled by the computer's software (as shown in the photograph).

*Sound can be produced from a computer using loudspeakers and controlled on screen.*

## *Storing sounds*

The loudness of sounds varies on a smooth, continuous scale, between very quiet and very loud. In the same way, the **pitch** of sound varies continuously between very low and very high. This kind of continuous variation is called **analogue** variation. When values change in distinct steps rather than on a smooth scale we say that the values are **digital**. Computers can only work with digital values, so to handle sound using a computer we must change the pattern of the sound from analogue to digital values when the sound is input and its pattern is stored. The stored digital values can be used to generate sound from the computer, through loudspeakers. Figure 7.1 shows the analogue pattern of loudness of a sound over a fraction of a second, and Figure 7.2 shows the digital pattern of the same sound. You can see the continuous lines in the first pattern and the separate steps in the second pattern.

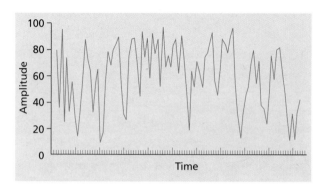

**Figure 7.1** *A sound signal with continuously varying amplitude (loudness). This is an analogue signal.*

**Figure 7.2** *The same sound as in the last figure, shown as a digital sound.*

Many modern computers have a speaker built in to the system. Sound can be generated through this speaker, but the quality of the sound often leaves a lot to be desired. Better quality sounds can be produced by **sampling** the sound, storing the samples on disk and then playing them back – but standard computers don't always have the parts to do this. Even a short sound sequence needs a lot of stored data. Storing very large samples can take up a vast amount of memory and disk space. Playing back these samples needs extra **chips** and circuits inside the computer and better speakers than are usually built into a standard computer system.

Computers that have special sound hardware can store sounds inputted through a microphone and can play them back. Software can be used to combine and distort these samples in lots of ways to make new sounds which can be played back through high-quality speakers. Sampled sounds are often used in computer games, but you only hear them properly if you play the game on a computer with the extra hardware and speakers.

## ◼ *Sampling sound*

You can sample sound by connecting a microphone to the computer system and creating the sounds you want. This has some limitations, because any stray sound in the room – like a chair being moved, someone coughing, or even breathing noises – will also be picked up and stored by the computer.

If a computer has the right kind of connection (a **MIDI interface**) then, with the right software, sound produced on an electronic keyboard can be sampled directly, cutting out the problem of stray noise. When

*Music recording studio sampling.*

you sample a sound the analogue values of the sound are converted into digital values for the computer to store. This has to be done many thousands of times a second to make sure that the quality of the sound is as much like the original as possible – this is why sampling needs so much memory in the computer and storage space on disk.

Any kind of sound can be sampled using a microphone – not just speech and music. Once a sound has been sampled and its pattern stored, it can be replayed by converting the digital pattern stored on disk back into sound played through a speaker system.

# Mixing and distortion

Sounds that have been sampled can be altered in various ways by using special computer software. It is possible to **mix** several different samples. For example, if you need a farmyard sound you could sample pig, sheep and cow sounds separately then combine them to make a background noise of animals. You could combine this mix with other sounds (such as tractor noises or speech) to produce the final effect of a busy farmyard.

One obvious use of sound mixing is in producing sound tracks for films. Special effects, such as noises for aliens and dinosaurs, have been produced for many films by mixing and **distorting** sampled sounds. Mixing and some distortion is used in recording music as well, producing effects that can't be produced on any musical instrument.

## ■ *Sequencing*

**S**equencing sounds is deciding the order in which to play sound samples. In the example of the farm we used earlier, you might not want all the sounds at the same time – you might want the animal noises first, then the tractor and the farmer. You can set up this sequence by setting the order in which the samples are to be used. You can repeat very short sequences to produce special effects as well – for example, repeating the middle section of a short squeal several times will turn it into a long howl.

## ■ *Speech recognition*

**S**oftware is now available which will let you speak into a microphone and turn what you say into text in a word processed document. You need to 'train' the software to recognise your voice and the sound patterns of different words. This method of inputting text is easier for some people than typing. The computer will sometimes put the wrong word into the document but the software is getting better all the time.

## ■ *Working with sound*

**I**f you want to work with sound, you should check what the computer systems available to you can do. If the hardware can do what you want (and if the special software packages are available) you will be able to sample and store sounds and to combine and distort them. The sounds can then be played back as required. Multimedia software will let you attach particular stored sounds to pictures or actions.

## Summary

- Sounds can be sampled and stored using a computer system.
- Stored sounds can be replayed unchanged.
- Sound samples can be combined and altered to produce new sounds.
- Storage of sound data can take quite a lot of disk space because to get good quality the sound characteristics must be captured thousands of times a second.
- Getting good-quality sound out of a computer system requires extra hardware (such as speakers) and extra chips and circuits in the computer.

## SKILLS

When you have completed the work in this chapter, providing you have the right hardware and software, you should be able to:

- Sample sounds.
- Play back sampled sounds.
- Mix different sounds.
- Organise sequences of sounds.

### Questions

1 What is meant by:

   a sampling
   b distorting
   c mixing of sound?

2 How could sound be used effectively in each of the following situations?

   a In presenting information on screen about events at a school open day.
   b As part of a word-processing package.
   c As part of a multimedia presentation about zoo animals.

In each case explain what kind of sound you would want to use and how this sound would be produced.

# Communication with other computer systems

Communication between computer systems is becoming more and more important. This can range from using a Local Area Network to share the same hard disk drives and printer to sending Email messages across the world and down-loading information from the Internet.

## WHAT IS A NETWORK?

A network consists of computers that are able to communicate and the connections and hardware which allow this to happen. In a Local Area Network (LAN) cables are used to connect the networked computer to the main file-server. In a Wide Area Network (WAN) the computers are not joined by cables but use other kinds of communication link such as telephone lines or radio links. A local area network can be connected to a wide area network through a 'gateway'.

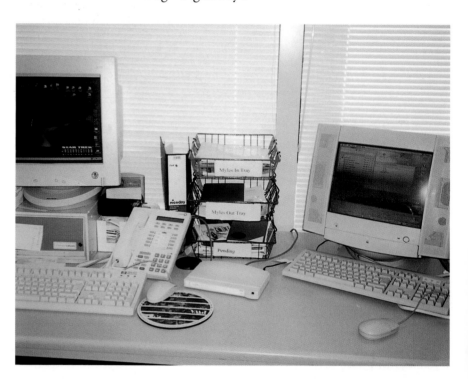

**Figure 8.1** *A Local Area Network*

## WHY HAVE A LOCAL AREA NETWORK?

If computers are connected to a local area network then there are lots of advantages for the people using the network.

- All the computers can share resources such as printers. This can mean that faster, better quality printing is available to everyone because one or two printers can be bought instead of lots of cheaper ones. It is important to know which printer your work is going to, otherwise you may have a problem finding it!
- Central backing store (hard disk drives) can be provided so all work can be saved in one place. This means you can load your work on any computer on the network.
- Software can be shared. This means that all the terminals can use the same software. Upgrading the software is easier too. Sharing software this way is not usually much cheaper than providing a copy for every machine because licences have to be bought for the number of copies needed.
- Central back-up will almost certainly take place at regular intervals. This means that you don't need to worry about doing your own back-up copies and you will be able to get your work back if you accidentally delete it.
- Data can be shared across the network so several people can work on the same project. For example, lots of people could write articles for a school magazine and save them in the same area. One person could then assemble each page, using the articles which had been saved. It is not usually possible to open the same document at the same time on two different computers although you can make an extra copy of it.
- If the data being shared is in a database then several people will be able to use the database at the same time but they won't be able to edit the same record at the same time. When a record is opened it is locked so other people can't try to edit it at the same time. As soon as changes have been made and saved the record is unlocked again.

- Local Email messages can be sent to people working at other computers. This can save a lot of walking about and ensures that messages do get to the right place. Unfortunately they may not be read by the person they are addressed to. Email messages are stored in a mail-box until they are opened. Some people are not very good at checking for mail.
- There may be a local **Intranet**. This has pages of information and works like the World Wide Web. The difference is that the pages can only be accessed over the local area network. As this doesn't involve phone links an intranet is free.

## WHAT ARE THE DISADVANTAGES?

Local area networks do have some problems associated with them.

- Network security can be a problem. If a virus gets onto one computer it is likely to spread quickly to all the computers because it will get onto the central backing store.
- Users of the network have to have user names and passwords. Sometimes they are not very good at keeping passwords secret or they use passwords which are easy to guess. This makes it easy for other people to log onto the network.
- If the main file-server fails then the work stored on the shared hard disk drives will not be accessible and it will not be possible to use network printers. Failure of the file-server does not damage the other computers on the network.
- Damage to cables will mean that some sections of the network cannot communicate with the rest. Exactly how bad the effect is depends on the way the network is connected.

## WIDE AREA NETWORKS

A wide area network (WAN) is not limited to one building. It can be world wide. If you have a connection to a wide area network you will be able to share data with people miles away.

The Internet is really a vast wide area network. These networks always involve external communication links and mostly this involves paying for the connection.

# The Internet

One of the most exciting and fastest growing applications of Information Technology within communications is the Internet. Currently there are over 30 million users and yet for many, it appears to be something which has developed 'overnight'. It has become known as the Information Superhighway.

## What is the Internet?

The Internet is not just one computer, but the biggest network in the world. It is in fact a network of networks, a group of thousands of smaller computer networks, worldwide, all linked together. Some of the computers on the Internet are small PCs whilst others are large supercomputers. Because the data held on any of these computers can be accessed from any other on the network, the Internet, therefore, holds a vast amount of information. The Prime Minister Tony Blair, amongst others, has called it 'the biggest library in the world'. The Internet then, is not a particular place but a worldwide collection of computers all with an Internet connection. These connections are usually telephone and cable links.

## How do you connect to the Internet?

There are two main ways in which a user can be connected into the network.

It is possible to have a permanent connection, and this may be the situation in some business organisations or universities. Many users, however, use a modem, which is a device which connects between the computer and the telephone line and converts the digital signal produced by the computer into an analogue signal which can be transmitted along normal voice-carrying telephone lines. These users pay a subscription to a service provider, which is an organisation offering connections to the Internet. These service providers have a link into the Internet which is often called a point of presence (PoP). For many users, it is important that they choose a service provider with a PoP near to them, as their modem has to dial up a connection to it and once connected (on-line), the user has to pay the cost of the telephone charges. A local rate call is therefore cheaper than a long distance one. Although the Internet itself is free, it can be quite costly to tap into – a monthly subscription to a service provider plus the cost of the telephone call for every second a user is on-line. The rate at which modems can convert the signals is now very important and whereas rates of 2.4 kilobits per second (Kbps) were the norm in the 1980s, nowadays users should not consider a modem which is slower than 34Kbps and preferably one which can handle 56Kbps. The faster the modem, the shorter the telephone calls to the PoP have to be.

There are many ways in which the Internet can be used. We shall concentrate on two of these, the World Wide Web and EMail.

# World Wide Web

When people talk about the Internet, they are usually referring to the World Wide Web. It is a collection of sets of pages of information called sites about almost any topic you can think of. These pages not only contain text but also pictures, sound, movies and animations.

In order for your computer to display these pages, some software called a web browser is needed. There are two main browsers in use: Netscape Navigator and Microsoft Internet Explorer.

Although these browsers look slightly different, they both work in the same way.

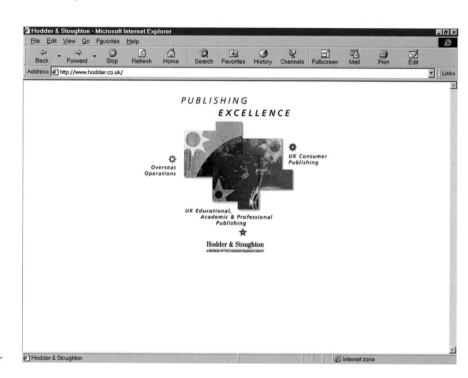

**Figure 8.2** *Microsoft Internet Explorer*

**Figure 8.3** *Netscape Navigator*

## HOW TO FIND A SITE

Every page on the Internet has its own unique address. This is called the Uniform Resource Locator or URL. If you know the URL of the site or page you are looking for, you can type this straight into the browser.

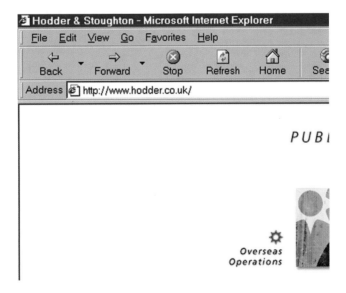

**Figure 8.4**

Here you can see we have typed in the URL *http://www.hodder.co.uk* Browsers will accept the URL typed without the http://, so we could have just typed *www.hodder.co.uk*

What makes the World Wide Web special is the fact that the pages it contains are not separate but connected together by links. These links are areas on a web page which, when clicked on using the mouse, take you to another page. Links can be recognised easily on a page. In text, they are usually a different colour to the rest of the text and underlined. Pictures and icons can also be links. When the cursor, which is normally an arrow, moves over a picture or icon which is a link it changes to a hand with a pointing finger.

Exploring the World Wide Web is called surfing.

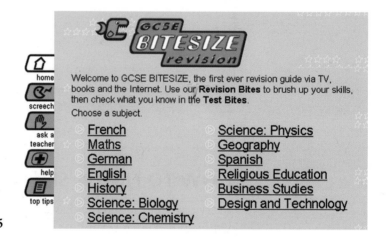

**Figure 8.5**

## SEARCHING THE WORLD WIDE WEB

Because the World Wide Web is made up of millions of sites, it is unlikely that you know the URLs of all the pages which contain information on the topic you are interested in.

By clicking on the search button on the toolbar of your browser you can use a special piece of software called a search engine.

A search engine asks you for keywords that describe what you are looking for and then comes up with a set of links to websites that contain your chosen words.

When you click on the search button on the toolbar, you will be offered a choice of search engines with names like Yahoo, Excite, Altavista, Lycos and Infoseek. Each one may produce different lists because of how it has found the websites which contain your chosen words.

Let us imagine we were looking for information about Alton Towers theme park.

We could type the words Alton Towers into the search box.

**Figure 8.6**

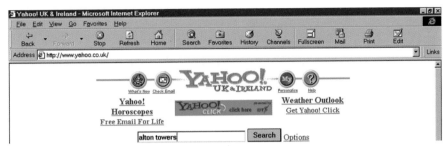

In this case we would obtain links to over 50000 documents which contain either the words alton or towers.

If we type the words using a mixture of upper and lower case letters e.g. Alton Towers the search will try to find documents which match the words exactly – i.e. Alton with a capital A. If we type the words using only lower case letters e.g. alton towers then the search engine will find documents containing those words regardless of whether they are all in lower case, all in upper case or a mixture of both.

By using double quotes around a number of keywords the search engines will only find the words in the order that they are in those quotes.

So if we type "alton towers" the search engine only lists links to documents where the word alton comes before towers.

**Figure 8.7**

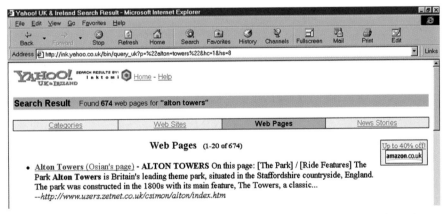

As you can see, by searching this way we only have 674 pages rather than the 50000 we obtained by searching without using the quotes.

## ADVANCED SEARCHING

If the lists of links to websites that we get from search engines are going to be useful to us, we need to keep the number of suggested pages down as well as making sure that they point us to relevant information. The only way of doing this is to carry out advanced searches.

Each search engine has slightly different rules for carrying out these advanced searches but the main possibilities are as follows:

## +and−

If you put a + in front of a word, documents will be found which contain that word.

For example,

## +handball+rules

will find documents which contain the word handball and also the word rules. This search would help you find out about the rules of handball rather than anything to do with handball.

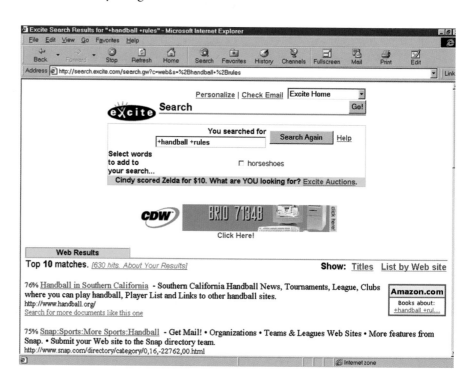

Figure 8.8

## handball+rules

would give a list of links to documents which will have the word rules in their text but will not necessarily be about handball.

If we place a − in front of a word, documents will be found which do not contain that word

For example

## +handball−rules

would give a list of links to documents which contain the word handball but miss out those which contain the word rules. This search could be used to find out more about handball in general rather than its rules.

## AND, OR, AND NOT

The word AND is used to combine keywords. All words joined by AND must be contained in the document for it to be listed in the results of the search.

For example, if you wish to research the exploration of planet Mars by the spacecraft surveyor then you could type

mars AND surveyor

Into the search box. The resulting list would give you links to websites which contain both the words mars and surveyor.

**Figure 8.9**

The word OR is also used to combine keywords. At least one of the words joined by OR must be contained in the document for it to be listed in the results of the search.

For example,

cat OR dog

would produce a list of websites with documents containing either the word cat, the word dog or both.

OR is often used to link words which have a similar meaning.

For example, if you were researching cycling, searching for

cycling OR biking

would give you a wider choice of websites.

AND NOT is also used to combine keywords. Documents found cannot contain the word following the AND NOT. Using

football AND NOT america

would list websites containing the word football but would not include those containing the word america.

## BRACKETS

The use of brackets in searches is exactly the same as they are used in Maths, that is to make more complex searches by means of grouping words together. The groupings in brackets are carried out first.

For example,

mars AND (surveyor OR pathfinder)

would produce a list of websites with documents containing the word mars and either the word surveyor or the word pathfinder or both.

Figure 8.10

## WILDCARDS

The character * can be used to stand for any character or set of characters. It is called a wildcard.

For example, typing

auto*

would produce a list of links to websites with documents containing the words automobile, autograph, automatic, autopsy amongst many others.

## TITLES

Rather than search documents or websites for keywords, it is possible to simply search the titles of documents or websites for those words. If the words are important to that document or website then they may well be contained in the title. This is done by typing t: before the keyword(s).

For example:

t: "blue peter"

would look for the words blue peter in the titles.

**Figure 8.11**

# Email

Electronic mail or Email as it is generally called is a way of sending messages using the Internet. It is one of the most useful parts of the Internet.

It is a way of communicating on a world wide basis and is very fast as well as being inexpensive. To be able to use Email, you need an Email account (usually with a service provider). You will be given a unique Email address. An example address would be *jsmith@adsupplies.co.uk*

The way Email works is simple. You start up some Email software which you may be able to do from your web browser or else separately.

You use this software to prepare the message which can include pictures or even other files, as well as text.

You tag the message with the Email address of the person or place to which it has to be sent.

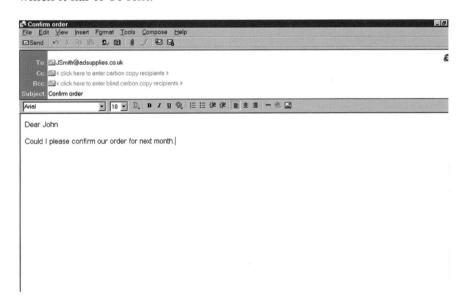

**Figure 8.12**

This can all be done when you are not connected to the Internet to save telephone charges.

When you are ready to send the message, it is simply a matter of connecting to the Internet, clicking on send and away it goes.

Because the time it takes to transmit the message is only a few seconds, the cost of sending mail is cheap and costs the same whether the message is sent to someone in the same town or on the other side of the world.

Any messages sent to you are usually stored on a computer at your service provider and stay there until you download them to your computer.

**Figure 8.13**

Using the software shown in Figure 8.13, this be done by clicking on the 'send and receive' button on the toolbar.

Email can be used for all sorts of reasons, both business and pleasure, in fact for exactly the same reasons that you would want to send a letter.

With Email on the Internet, it is also possible to join mailing lists. This is a way of allowing a number of people to talk about a subject using Email and there are hundreds of different mailing lists covering a wide variety of topics. You would join the list and when you send a message to it, everyone else on the list receives a copy of it.

You can also subscribe to mailing lists free of charge and receive regular updates on particular issues.

You can now see why Email is one of the most popular and important uses of the Internet.

# Summary

- Local area networks are confined to a small area and are connected by cables.

- Wide area networks can extend over many miles.

- There are no costs involved in communicating using a local area network

- A wide area network usually uses phone lines and this means that communicating costs money.

- An intranet is the local area network equivalent of the internet.

- The Internet is a huge Wide Area network.

- An Internet browser lets you access the internet on a computer with a suitable connection.

- You need to specify searches carefully to find what you want on the internet as there are lots of web pages.

- You can save the addresses (URLs) of sites you visit often so you can go straight to them.

## Questions

1 A software company sends information to its customers by personalised letter.

   a The company is considering using electronic mail to send information to its customers. Describe the process of sending and receiving electronic mail. (MEG)

2 A building firm buys a computer system and some software to help run the business. As the business expands they get two more computer systems for the office. The owner of the business wants to use the same word processing package on all three machines.

   a Explain why he should buy extra copies of the software.
   b He wants to keep records of his customers on the three computers and thinks it would be a good idea to install a network.
      i Give **three** advantages to the staff of having the computers connected to a local area network (LAN).
      ii Give **one** possible disadvantage (other than cost) of having the network installed. (NEAB)

3 The Internet is a world-wide network containing large amounts of data.

   a Give **three** distinct ways in which Internet access might be useful to a journalist working from home.
   b There have been suggestions that information available on the Internet should be controlled.
      i Explain why such control might be a good idea.
      ii Explain why such control might be opposed. (NEAB)

# Spreadsheets

You can use a **spreadsheet** to carry out calculations. A spreadsheet is useful because you can do lots of calculations and use the answers you get to work out other things in the same spreadsheet. Once you have set up your spreadsheet you can change some of the numbers and it will work out the new answers for you. When you have all your answers on the screen you can print out your work, with all the headings and explanations you have included. You can save your work on disk so you can finish it later or in case you want to use the same spreadsheet for new sets of data.

## ■ *Spreadsheet basics*

A spreadsheet is a grid, which looks like a table, divided into columns and rows. Each **cell** in the grid can be identified by the column it is in and the row it is in – this is called the **cell address** (you can see this in Figure 9.1). For example, the address B3 means the cell is in column B and in the third row.

| | A | B | C | D | E | F | G | H |
|---|---|---|---|---|---|---|---|---|
| 1 | | | | | | | | |
| 2 | | | | | | | | |
| 3 | | | | | | | | |
| 4 | | | | | | | | |
| 5 | | | | | | | | |

**Figure 9.1** *An empty spreadsheet, showing columns, rows and cells*

Cells can contain text, numbers or **formulae,** You use text for headings and labels to make things clear. The numbers you put into the spreadsheet are used to carry out calculations. You use formulae to tell the computer how to calculate the answers you want. The formula contains the address of each cell used in the calculation and any fixed numbers you need – you can see an example of a formula in Figure 9.2.

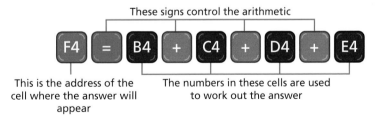

These signs control the arithmetic

This is the address of the cell where the answer will appear

The numbers in these cells are used to work out the answer

**Figure 9.2** *An example of a spreadsheet formula*

The formula in Figure 9.2 adds together the contents of cells B4, C4, D4 and E4 and puts the answer in cell F4. Arithmetic in spreadsheets uses these signs:

- $+$    for addition
- $-$    for subtraction

**Q**

**What three items can a cell in a spreadsheet contain? Give an explanation and an example of each of these items.**

**What do we mean by a cell address? Give an example of a cell address from the spreadsheet package you use at school.**

\*   for multiplication
/   for division
^   for raising to a power (exponentiation) – for example, 2^3 means $2^3$

If you put part of the formula in brackets, that part will be worked out before any other parts.

Figure 9.3 is a spreadsheet that has been used to work out how much television time was used for different types of programme in one week. The printout shows the formulae instead of the answers.

Figure 9.4 is the same spreadsheet, printed out to show the answers.

**Figure 9.3** *Spreadsheet of television programmes, showing the formulae*

**Figure 9.4** *The same spreadsheet as in Figure 9.3, with the answers included in the printout.*

# What your spreadsheet package can do

Different spreadsheet packages have different ways of showing what you want to put in a cell. For the spreadsheet package you are using, find out how to:

- put text into cells
- put numbers in a cell
- put a formula in a cell
- change the width of a column
- duplicate a formula
- print your spreadsheet.

You will probably find it useful to know how to duplicate a formula down a column or across a row. In our television programmes spreadsheet (Figure 9.3) the formula was put in cell F4. In the other rows we also needed to add up cells in the same columns as for F4 so we copied the formula down the column in a way that made the package change the row number for each row down the spreadsheet. So, in row 5 the formula became:

$$F5 = B5 + C5 + D5 + E5.$$

We can also copy cell addresses as they are.

Learning how to copy will save you lots of typing and, if you have complicated formulae, will help you to avoid mistakes.

You will need to know how to print your spreadsheet to show both data and formulae, so that people can see how you worked out your answers.

As you work with your spreadsheet package you will discover more about what it can do. You will be able to:

- change the cell format so that the contents are centred or on the left or the right
- make answers appear with a fixed number of decimal places
- you may be able to select data to produce graphs and charts that can be printed out.

# Spreadsheet functions

Most spreadsheet packages can do much more than the simple arithmetic we have described so far. It will have a number of different **functions** it can carry out.

- The SUM function adds up the values in a range of cells. It looks like this:

=SUM(B3:B15)

This is much easier to write than the alternative:

=B3 + B4 + B5 + B6 + B7 + B8 + B9 + B10 + B11 + B12 + B13 + B14 + B15

- The AVERAGE function works with a range of cells and gives the average of the values they contain.
- The COUNT function counts up how many cells in a range have data in them.
- The IF function is very useful. It allows for different answers depending on the value in a particular cell. This spreadsheet uses these formulae:

Cell F3 contains the formula =AVERAGE(B3:E3). This works out the average mark for Susan Clark.

Cell G3 contains the formula =IF (F3>=70,"A","B"). This checks whether cell F3 contains a value greater than or equal to 70. If it does then it puts the letter A in cell G3 otherwise it puts B in cell G3.

| | Pupil | English | Maths | Science | French | Average | Grade |
|---|---|---|---|---|---|---|---|
| 1 | | | | | | | |
| 2 | | | | | | | |
| 3 | Clarke Susan | 53 | 60 | 51 | 55 | 54.75 | B |
| 4 | Donnelly Katie | 60 | 54 | 63 | 70 | 61.75 | B |
| 5 | Muir Alexandra | 57 | 72 | 77 | 51 | 64.25 | B |
| 6 | O'Brien Liam | 65 | 70 | 60 | 71 | 66.50 | B |
| 7 | Osu Mary | 80 | 87 | 90 | 76 | 83.25 | A |
| 8 | Smith Paul | 75 | 65 | 72 | 73 | 71.25 | A |

**Figure 9.5** *A spreadsheet used to calculate average marks and grades. The AVERAGE function is used to work out the mean mark for each pupil. An IF function is used to decide which grade to give*

# ■*Designing and setting up your own spreadsheet*

Before you can set up your spreadsheet you will need to think about what answers you want to produce.

## STEP 1

Decide the questions that need to be answered and the calculations you will need to carry out to get these answers.

## STEP 2

Work out what data you will need to calculate the answers to your questions and collect the data.

You will probably need to do some research to collect the information that you need in order to get this data. In our spreadsheet example, the details about programme length and type were collected from television magazines.

## STEP 3

Design the layout of the spreadsheet – you will need to work out what headings are needed and how wide the columns will have to be (remember headings tend to need more room than numbers).

When you start to design the layout it is a good idea to plan it out on squared paper because lots of layouts are possible and you need to decide which one will work best. You don't need to put in all the data but you should show what goes where and how to **format** it. Formatting includes the position of what goes in the cell and the number of decimal places. Put formulae in where they are needed but, where you will duplicate the formula all the way down a column, don't bother to write the formula in every cell in that column.

| | *A* | *B* | *C* | *D* | *E* | *F* | *G* | *H* |
|---|---|---|---|---|---|---|---|---|
| 1 | DAY | CHANNEL | SPORT | FILM | SOAPS | CHILDRENS | NEWS | HOURS TRANSMITTED |
| 2 | | | | | | | | |
| 3 | Monday | BBC1 | All data in these columns is numeric, uses 1 decimal place and is right justified | | | | | |
| 4 | | BBC2 | | | | | | |
| 5 | | ITV | | | | | | |
| 6 | | CH4 | | | | | | |
| 7 | | | | | | | | |
| 8 | Tuesday | BBC1 | | | | | | |
| 9 | | BBC2 | | | | | | |
| 10 | | ITV | | | | | | |
| 11 | | CH4 | | | | | | |
| 12 | | | | | | | | |
| 13 | Wednesday | BBC1 | | | | | | |
| 14 | | BBC2 | | | | | | |
| 15 | | ITV | | | | | | |
| 16 | | CH4 | | | | | | |
| 17 | | | | | | | | |
| 18 | Thursday | BBC1 | | | | | | |
| 19 | | BBC2 | | | | | | |
| 20 | | ITV | | | | | | |
| 21 | | CH4 | | | | | | |
| 22 | | | | | | | | |
| 23 | Friday | BBC1 | | | | | | |
| 24 | | BBC2 | | | | | | |
| 25 | | ITV | | | | | | |
| 26 | | CH4 | | | | | | |
| 27 | | | | | | | | |
| 28 | Saturday | BBC1 | | | | | | |
| 29 | | BBC2 | | | | | | |
| 30 | | ITV | | | | | | |
| 31 | | CH4 | | | | | | |
| 32 | | | | | | | | |
| 33 | Sunday | BBC1 | | | | | | |
| 34 | | BBC2 | | | | | | |
| 35 | | ITV | | | | | | |
| 36 | | CH4 | | | | | | |
| 37 | | | | | | | | |
| 38 | | | | | | | | |
| 39 | | | | | | | | |
| 40 | Total | | =SUM(C3:C36) | Duplicate formulae across (relative) | | | | |
| 41 | | | | | | | | |
| 42 | % OF TOTAL TRANSMISSION | | =SUM(C40/$H$40)*100) | Duplicate this formula across as well – note that cell H40 is an ASBSOLUTE cell address and won't be changed. Cell C40 will be changed as it is duplicated. | | | | |
| 43 | | | | | | | | |
| 44 | | | | | | | | |
| 45 | | | | | | | | |

**Figure 9.6** *The design for the television programme spreadsheet*

In designing your spreadsheet think about whether the data is grouped so that it is clear and whether it's easy to see the answers.

If you plan to draw graphs or charts with some data, keep the data and headings in groups – you won't be able to use data for a graph if the data is scattered all over the spreadsheet.

The design for the television programme spreadsheet can be seen in Figure 9.6.

## STEP 4

Set up the spreadsheet on the computer. The first thing to do is to adjust the **column widths** so that everything will fit in. When you've done this, put in the headings – these will help you get the data in the right places.

Set up the formulae in the cells and save your spreadsheet on disk. Don't forget to give it a sensible name and make a note of the name you use.

Now put in the data. If your spreadsheet is set to automatically recalculate, so that it always works out answers straight away, the answers will appear in the cells with formulae in them. Once you have put all the data, save your work again with a different name.

You can now use the spreadsheet to produce any graphs you need. The bar chart in Figure 9.7 was produced from our television programmes spreadsheet. It shows how the time used for each type of programme differs for different channels.

You will probably also need to print out the spreadsheet to show what you have found out.

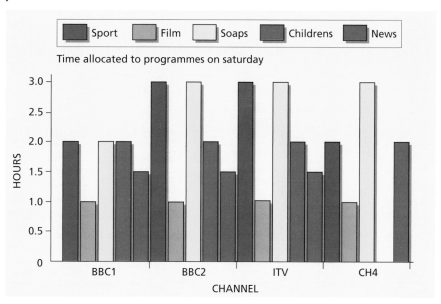

**Figure 9.7**  *A bar chart produced from the database, showing how the time for each type of programme differs*

# Summary

- Spreadsheets can be used to carry out calculations.
- In a spreadsheet the **data** is entered by the user.
- A spreadsheet contains formulae – the rules for working out the answers from the data.
- Spreadsheets also contain text to put the data into context so that it becomes **information** for the user.
- In some packages, data from spreadsheets can be used to produce graphs and charts.

## SKILLS

When you have completed the work in this chapter you should be able to:

- Design a simple spreadsheet.
- Use your spreadsheet package to set up a spreadsheet.
- Put data into your spreadsheet.
- Read the answers from your spreadsheet.
- Produce graphs and charts from spreadsheet data.

# Questions

1 How is a single location in a spreadsheet identified?

2 The spreadsheet below is used to store details of stock in a shop's stock control room system:

| | A | B | C | D | E | F | G | H |
|---|---|---|---|---|---|---|---|---|
| 1 | STOCK | NAME | SIZE | STOCK | SELLING | VALUE | MINIMUM | NO. ABOVE |
| 2 | NO. | | | LEVEL | PRICE | | STOCK | MINIMUM |
| 3 | | | | | | | LEVEL | |
| 4 | | | | | | | | |
| 5 | 0234 | Baked beans | 420 g | 127 | 0.36 | 45.72 | 24 | 103 |
| 6 | 0245 | Beefburgers | 12 pack | 36 | 1.98 | 71.28 | 12 | 24 |
| 7 | 0367 | Lentils | 500 g | 45 | 0.45 | 20.25 | 12 | 33 |
| 8 | 0478 | Long grain rice | 1000 g | 70 | 1.46 | 102.2 | 25 | 45 |
| 9 | 0579 | Peaches | 550 g | 36 | 0.78 | 28.08 | 12 | 24 |

a Which locations would have to be changed if a new delivery of baked beans arrived?

b Name two locations containing numbers worked out using formulae.

c It would be useful if the spreadsheet showed the total value of the stock. How would you make it do this?

d Which location would you change if the price of rice went up by 5p? Which locations would change as a result of this?

3 A spreadsheet is used to process data about temperatures for a year.

| | A | B | C | D |
|---|---|---|---|---|
| 1 | Month | Minimum temperature | Maximum temperature | Average temperature |
| 2 | | | | |
| 3 | January | −6 | 4 | average (b3:c3) |
| 4 | February | −3 | 5 | |
| 5 | March | 11 | 7 | |
| 6 | April | 3 | 9 | |
| 7 | May | 4 | 11 | |
| 8 | June | 7 | 15 | |
| 9 | July | 9 | 20 | |
| 10 | August | 8 | 25 | |
| 11 | September | 7 | 18 | |
| 12 | October | 6 | 12 | |
| 13 | November | 3 | 11 | |
| 14 | December | 1 | 8 | |

a Cell D3 shows how the average temperature for January is calculated. After putting the formula in D3, describe the best way of putting the formula into D4 to D14.

b Write down **one** cell which contains a data entry error.

c Describe how you would create a graph which showed how the minimum temperatures changed over the year.

4 A spreadsheet is being set up to show the cost of several school field trips. Describe the main features of a spreadsheet which will allow the data to be analysed to find the lowest costs. (MEG)

5 A group of friends who live in the North East of England regularly go to pop concerts. Next year they are planning to go to five concerts. Not everyone wants to go to all of the concerts. Below is part of the spreadsheet that is used to work out the cost of each trip. This is produced once it is known how many people will be going to each concert and the cost of the tickets.

| | A | B | C | D | E | F | G |
|---|---|---|---|---|---|---|---|
| 1 | Group | Venue | Travel costs | No. of | Travel costs | Cost of 1 | Total cost |
| 2 | | | for car | people in | for 1 person | concert | of trip for |
| 3 | | | | the car | | ticket | one person |
| 4 | | | | | | | |
| 5 | Oasis | London | £60.00 | 4 | £15.00 | £20.00 | £35.00 |
| 6 | Spice Girls | Birmingham | £40.00 | 4 | £10.00 | £18.00 | £28.00 |
| 7 | Blur | Newcastle | £15.00 | 3 | £5.00 | £17.00 | £22.00 |
| 8 | Hanson | Manchester | £30.00 | 2 | £15.00 | £15.00 | £30.00 |
| 9 | Peter Andre | Glasgow | £40.00 | 2 | £20.00 | £15.00 | £35.00 |

a The travel cost for the car for the trip to Manchester was wrongly entered. The cost should have been **£35 not £30**. Which **cell** in the spreadsheet must be changed?

b Which **two other cells** would change automatically as a result of this change?

c What **formula** would be in the cell E5?

d Name **one** other cell, in another column, that contains a **different** formula.

e Last year the friends used a calculator to work out their costs. Give **three advantages** of using a spreadsheet like the one given above, compared with their old manual method.

6 'Pave and Turf' are a firm of landscape gardeners. They design gardens after talking to customers about their needs. In order to give customers a quote for the cost of landscaping their garden, they use a spreadsheet package on their computer system.

You can see an outline of a spreadsheet they use below:

|    | A | B | C | D | E |
|----|---|---|---|---|---|
| 1  | Article | Unit | Cost of | Number of | Total Cost |
| 2  | | | 1 unit | units needed | of articles |
| 3  | Turf | per square metre | | | |
| 4  | Patio stones | per stone | | | |
| 5  | Bricks | per brick | | | |
| 6  | Top soil | per 1000 kg | | | |
| 7  | Sand | per 50 kg | | | |
| 8  | Cement | per 50 kg | | | |
| 9  | Gravel | per 50 kg | | | |
| 10 | Compost | per 50 kg | | | |
| 11 | Labour | per person hour | | | |
| 12 | | | Total Cost | excluding VAT | |
| 13 | | | VAT at 17.5% | of Total Cost | |
| 14 | | | Final Cost | including VAT | |

This spreadsheet package has rules for entering formulae. These are as follows:

**Each formula must start with an equals sign.**

**Symbols used are**    **+ for addition**
**− for subtraction**
**\* for multiplication**
**/ for division**

For example
=**P7 + Q8** is a formula which would add the value in cell P7 to the value in cell Q8
=**R9 \* 3.2** is a formula which would multiply the value in cell R9 by 3.2
To add the values in a range of cells together, the following formula would be used:
=**SUM (first cell in range: last cell in range)**
For example
=**SUM (T5:T9)** would add together the values in cells T5, T6, T7, T8 and T9

a   **Using the above rules**, state the formula which would be contained in the following cells:
  (i)   E4
  (ii)  E12
  (iii) E13
  (iv)  E14

b   Before this spreadsheet was produced, it had to be designed. Many items have to be thought about during this design stage. Any formulae required is one such item. Give **four other** items which have to be considered during the design stage of a spreadsheet.

# Using Spreadsheets for Modelling

## ■ *What is a computer model?*

A computer model contains data and rules. The rules control the way in which the model works. They are instructions for carrying out calculations, or conditions when particular calculations should be carried out. The model can be of a situation or a process. You can't use a spreadsheet to make a scale model of an object but you can use it to predict how that object will behave in certain situations. For example if you wanted to build a very strong container you could make a cardboard model to show its shape, but this model wouldn't be any use for predicting what would happen if the container fell off a lorry. A spreadsheet model of the container could contain data about the material the container is made from and rules (formulae) about how it would react to impact.

## ■ *Why use computer models?*

We use computer models to find out what will happen when we change a situation – without actually having to make these changes. For instance, we could investigate the effect of making the container walls different thickness without having to make lots of different containers and drop them off lorries.

This type of modelling has a number of advantages:

1  It's much cheaper to set up a computer model than to build a whole system for testing.
2  You can make changes quickly and easily in a computer model to find out what happens if the situation changes.
3  You can repeat your tests as often as you need to.
4  You can model dangerous situations safely (like testing car designs by 'crashing' them, without actually crashing a car).
5  If a test using a simulation or model goes badly wrong the consequences aren't disastrous – no-one gets hurt and it's not too expensive to try again.

**But**
You must remember that the computer model is not the real thing – a computer model can never *prove* that a system will work the same way in the real world. The answers or results that we get are only as reliable as the model we've created, and if we try to model very complex situations we

can never take into account all the factors. This is especially true if humans are involved in the situation – for example a computer model of the operation of the Stock Market will probably be unreliable because the humans involved in share dealing often react in unpredictable ways.

## Types of computer model

Computer models include:

- *Mathematical models* using spreadsheet software – these are often used for modelling financial situations.
- *Simulation modelling* where the model (the simulator) is as close to the real thing as possible – like the flight simulators used in training pilots. (More about simulators in Chapter 11.)

## Constructing a costing spreadsheet

In this section you are going to learn how to construct and use a simple spreadsheet model. We will take it step by step.

### STEP 1: DESCRIBE THE SITUATION TO BE MODELLED

The example we will use here is a financial model which will let you find out the cost of making a single portion of cake.

### STEP 2: DECIDE WHAT QUESTIONS YOU WANT TO ANSWER

You want to find out:

- How cutting the cake into smaller or bigger pieces would affect the cost of a portion.
- How changing prices of ingredients affects the cost of a portion.
- How a change in energy costs affects the cost of a portion.

You could use the spreadsheet to answer other questions as well – can you think of more?

**Q**

Explain what we mean by a computer model.

Write down three different types of computer model. For each type give an example of a situation where it is used.

List four reasons why using computer models is better than using real systems to test different situations.

| | A | B | C | D | E | F | G |
|---|---|---|---|---|---|---|---|
| | | | **Recipe Costing Sheet** | | | | |
| 1 | | | | | | | |
| 2 | | | | | | | |
| 3 | *Recipe for* | Fresh Cream Sponge Cake | | | | | |
| 4 | | | | | | | |
| 5 | *Number of portions* | | 8 | | | | |
| 6 | | | | | | | |
| 7 | Ingredient | Pack size | | Cost of | Amount | | Cost of this |
| 8 | | | | pack | needed | | amount |
| 9 | | | | | | | |
| 10 | margarine | | 500 g | 0.58 | 100 g | | =D10/B10*E10 |
| 11 | sugar | | 1000 g | 0.82 | 100 g | | =D11/B11*E11 |
| 12 | eggs | | 6 eggs | 0.72 | 1 egg | | =D12/B12*E12 |
| 13 | S. R. flour | | 1500 g | 0.56 | 125 g | | =D13/B13*E13 |
| 14 | milk | | 1000 ml | 0.38 | 45 ml | | =D14/B14*E14 |
| 15 | cocoa | | 125 g | 0.62 | 45 g | | =D15/B15*E15 |
| 16 | double cream | | 142 ml | 0.39 | 142 ml | | =D16/B16*E16 |
| 17 | | | | | | | |
| 18 | Other costs | | | | | | |
| 19 | | | | | | | |
| 20 | Cooking time | | 45.00 Mins | | | | |
| 21 | Power used | =1/60*B20 | Units | | | | |
| 22 | Cost per unit | | 0.0812 | | | | |
| 23 | Cost of baking | =B21*B22 | | | | | |
| 24 | | | | | | | |
| 25 | Cost per portion | =(SUM(G10: G16)+B23)/C5 | | | | | |

**Figure 10.1** *A financial model for making one slice of cake.*

## STEP 3: COLLECT THE INFORMATION YOU NEED TO GET THE DATA FOR THE SPREADSHEET

You need:

- A list of the ingredients in the cake.
- The amount of each ingredient you need.
- How much a pack of each ingredient costs.
- The size of each of the packs you would have to buy.
- The cost of a unit of electricity or gas.
- The number of portions of cake you expect to make.

You will find the ingredients list and quantities you need in a recipe book, the pack sizes and prices in your local supermarket and how much the electricity costs by looking at an electricity bill.

## STEP 4: WORK OUT THE RULES FOR YOUR MODEL

You will use the rules that you work out to construct the formulae when you design the actual spreadsheet.

This model doesn't have too many rules.

**Rule 1**   The cost of ingredients in the cake is:

$$\frac{cost\ of\ the\ pack \times amount\ used}{amount\ in\ the\ pack}$$

**Rule 2** The total cost of ingredients is the sum of the cost of each separate ingredient.

**Rule 3** Power used is:

*rating of oven in kW × cooking time in hours*

**Rule 4** Cost of baking is:

*power used × cost of a unit of power*

**Rule 5** Cost of a portion is:

$$\frac{(total\ cost\ of\ ingredients\ +\ cost\ of\ baking)}{number\ of\ portions\ made}$$

## STEP 5: DESIGN THE LAYOUT OF THE SPREADSHEET

It makes sense to plan out your spreadsheet on squared paper (just as you did when planning database reports in Chapter 3).

You must work out what headings you need so that your spreadsheet makes sense to anyone reading it. You should decide where all the data

**Figure 10.2** *The design for a spreadsheet to work out how much it would cost to produce a cake.*

| | A | B | C | D | E | F | G |
|---|---|---|---|---|---|---|---|
| 1 | | | | | | | |
| 2 | | | *Recipe Costing Sheet* | | | | |
| 3 | Recipe for | Text data | | | | | title runs across all cells – bold and underlined |
| 4 | | | | | | | |
| 5 | Number of portions | | name of recipe | | | | |
| 6 | | | | | | | Cost of this amount |
| 7 | Ingredient | Pack size | | Cost of pack | Amount needed | | |
| 8 | | | | | | | |
| 9 | | | | | | | |
| 10 | | | | | | | DIO/BIO*E10 |
| 11 | | Data here is numeric using no decimal places and justified right | | Numeric data, two decimal places, right justified | Numeric data, no decimal places, right justified | Data here is text for units | Duplicate down (relative) |
| 12 | Data here is text, justified left | | Data here is text for units | | | | |
| 13 | | | | | | | |
| 14 | | | | | | | |
| 15 | | | | | | | |
| 16 | | | | | | | |
| 17 | | | | | | | |
| 18 | Other costs | | | | | | |
| 19 | | | | | | | Circled headings in italics |
| 20 | Cooking time | (Numeric data) | | | | | Column widths: |
| 21 | Power used | (Numeric data) | | | | | A 18 |
| 22 | Cost per unit | (Numeric data) | | | | | B 5 - may need more |
| 23 | Cost of baking | =B21*B22 | | | | | C 4 |
| 24 | | | | | | | D 8 |
| 25 | Cost per portion | =(SUM(G10:G16)+B23)/C5 | | | | | E 7 |
| 26 | | | | | | | F 4 |
| 27 | | | Whole formula goes in cell B25 | | | | G 12 |
| 28 | This heading in bold or underlined | | | | | | Note: B2 - could use a formula here: |
| 29 | | | | | | | 1/60*B20 as oven has a 1KW rating |

will go on the spreadsheet. As you decide what goes in each column, you will also have to think about how wide the columns should be (remember that headings usually need more space than numbers). Show where you will put the data but don't bother to write it all in on the plan.

You need to decide where in each cell you want your text and numbers to appear – you can justify it left or right or you can have the cell contents centred (look back at Chapter 4 for what these terms mean). You also need to decide on the number of decimal places you want displayed. If your quantities are in grams and millilitres then you can display these numbers as whole numbers, but the cells with costs in them will need to display two decimal places.

If you want to include units in your spreadsheet you will have to put them in separate columns next to the numbers. If you try to put them in with the numbers the package will treat the cell contents as text and won't work out the answers correctly. Once you have decided on the layout of your spreadsheet you can work out the formulae you need. You couldn't do this before because the formulae need cell addresses.

You can see one way the recipe spreadsheet could be set up in Figure 10.2, but other layouts would work just as well. Notice that the formulae have already been put in to some of the cells. Cell G10 contains the formula:

$$= D10/B10*E10.$$

This is the formula for Rule 1 – the rule for working out how much the amount of a particular ingredient needed to make the cake costs. Cell D10 contains the cost of the packet of margarine. This is divided by the pack size, which is in B10, and is multiplied by the amount needed (which is in cell E10). In the design you only need to write this formula once because you'll be able to copy it into the other cells where it is needed by duplicating it down the column. The package will change the row numbers as it makes the extra copies.

The formula in cell B25 is different from the others. It uses a **function** to add up all the cells between G10 and G16. The function name is SUM. A function is a mathematical operation already set up in the package. This formula also contains brackets to make sure the arithmetic is done in the correct order.

## STEP 6: SET UP THE SPREADSHEET ON YOUR COMPUTER

Follow your design sheet carefully. You will need to alter column widths and cell formats to match your design. If you put your column headings in first, then put in the ingredients you will get all the data in the right cells. You should be able to lock column A so it doesn't disappear off the edge of the screen as you work across the spreadsheet – check the instructions for the package you're using to find out how to do this. Next, put in the formulae. When you have got this far you should save your work on disk with a sensible name.

### Recipe Costing Sheet

| | A | B | | C | D | E | F | G |
|---|---|---|---|---|---|---|---|---|
| 1 | | | | | | | | |
| 2 | | | | | | | | |
| 3 | *Recipe for* | Fresh Cream Sponge Cake | | | | | | |
| 4 | | | | | | | | |
| 5 | *Number of portions* | | | 8 | | | | |
| 6 | | | | | | | | |
| 7 | Ingredient | Pack size | | | Cost of | Amount | | Cost of this |
| 8 | | | | | pack | needed | | amount |
| 9 | | | | | | | | |
| 10 | margarine | | | 500 g | 0.58 | 100 g | | =D10/B10*E10 |
| 11 | sugar | | | 1000 g | 0.82 | 100 g | | =D11/B11*E11 |
| 12 | eggs | | | 6 eggs | 0.72 | 1 egg | | =D12/B12*E12 |
| 13 | S. R. flour | | | 1500 g | 0.56 | 125 g | | =D13/B13*E13 |
| 14 | milk | | | 1000 ml | 0.38 | 45 ml | | =D14/B14*E14 |
| 15 | cocoa | | | 125 g | 0.62 | 45 g | | =D15/B15*E15 |
| 16 | double cream | | | 142 ml | 0.39 | 142 ml | | =D16/B16*E16 |
| 17 | | | | | | | | |
| 18 | Other costs | | | | | | | |
| 19 | | | | | | | | |
| 20 | Cooking time | | | 45.00 Mins | | | | |
| 21 | Power used | =1/60*B20 | | Units | | | | |
| 22 | Cost per unit | | | 0.0812 | | | | |
| 23 | Cost of baking | =B21*B22 | | | | | | |
| 24 | | | | | | | | |
| 25 | Cost per portion | =(SUM(G10: G16)+B23)/C5 | | | | | | |

**Figure 10.3** *Recipe spreadsheet. Column B has had to be made wider to fit in the formula in cell B25, and column G has been expanded to fit in the formulae*

Now put in the data. The answers will probably appear straight away – if they don't you might have to give a command to make the spreadsheet do calculations. Sometimes the answers don't appear because the column isn't wide enough to fit them in.

You should check that the answers you're getting make sense – if they don't you've probably made a mistake in the formulae, or perhaps some of your numbers are being treated as text. When your spreadsheet is working properly, save it again with a different name.

You will probably want to print out your finished spreadsheet. You can print it with the answers and also with formulae. The recipe spreadsheets in Figures 10.3 and 10.4 show these two types of printout. In Figure 10.3 you can see that column B has had to be made wider to fit in the formula in cell B25, and column G needed to be wider to fit in the formulae in G10 to G16.

**Q**

Write down the stages you go through when you are constructing a computer model.

What checks should you carry out to ensure that a computer model is going to accurately reflect the situation or process you want it to?

## STEP 7: USE THE SPREADSHEET TO ANSWER THE QUESTIONS YOU STARTED WITH

- How would cutting the cake into smaller or bigger pieces affect the cost of a portion?
- How does changing the price of the ingredients affect the cost of a portion.
- Find out how a change in energy costs affects the cost of a portion.

In this spreadsheet some costs have a much bigger effect than others on the cost of each portion. What will have the biggest effect? What would you need to do if you decided to sell the cake and make a 25% profit?

### Recipe Costing Sheet

| | A | B | C | D | E | F | G |
|---|---|---|---|---|---|---|---|
| 1 | | | | | | | |
| 2 | | | | | | | |
| 3 | *Recipe for* | Fresh Cream Sponge Cake | | | | | |
| 4 | | | | | | | |
| 5 | *Number of portions* | | 8 | | | | |
| 6 | | | | | | | |
| 7 | Ingredient | Pack size | Cost of | Amount | | | Cost of this |
| 8 | | | pack | needed | | | amount |
| 9 | | | | | | | |
| 10 | margarine | 500 g | 0.58 | 100 g | | | 0.12 |
| 11 | sugar | 1000 g | 0.82 | 100 g | | | 0.08 |
| 12 | eggs | 6 eggs | 0.72 | 1 egg | | | 0.12 |
| 13 | S. R. flour | 15000 g | 0.56 | 125 g | | | 0.05 |
| 14 | milk | 1000 ml | 0.38 | 45 ml | | | 0.02 |
| 15 | cocoa | 125 g | 0.62 | 45 g | | | 0.22 |
| 16 | double cream | 142 ml | 0.39 | 142 ml | | | 0.39 |
| 17 | | | | | | | |
| 18 | Other costs | | | | | | |
| 19 | | | | | | | |
| 20 | Cooking time | | 45.00 | Mins | | | |
| 21 | Power used | | 0.75 | Units | | | |
| 22 | Cost per unit | | 0.0812 | | | | |
| 23 | Cost of baking | | 0.16 | | | | |
| 24 | | | | | | | |
| 25 | Cost per portion | | 0.13 | | | | |

**Figure 10.4** *The same spreadsheet, without the formulae.*

# Summary

- Spreadsheets are not the only way of constructing computer models.
- All models have rules.
- It is important to get these rules correct or the model won't work as you expect it to and the answers you get will be wrong.
- Even a simple model will probably have quite a lot of rules.
- If the data you use isn't accurate the model won't work as you expect and you will get misleading answers.

# Suggestions for modelling work

## SCIENCE

- Investigate the acceleration of a moving object.
- Investigate the effect of a temperature on the rate of a chemical reaction.
- Investigate the effect of light intensity on the volume of oxygen released during photosynthesis.

## TECHNOLOGY/DESIGN TECHNOLOGY

- Investigate the costs of project work, varying the materials used.

## ECONOMICS/BUSINESS STUDIES

- Create a model based on rules of supply and demand and look at the effects that changing prices will have.

## SKILLS

When you have completed the work in this chapter you should be able to:

- Identify a situation or process you could model using a spreadsheet.
- Decide what questions you could answer.
- Work out the data you would need to get these answers.
- Work out the rules for your model.
- Design and set up your spreadsheet model.
- Use your spreadsheet to answer the questions you started with.

## Questions

**1** A garden centre uses a spreadsheet to work out the cost of producing plants and how much they should be sold for.

|   | A | B | C | D | E | F | G | H | I |
|---|---|---|---|---|---|---|---|---|---|
| 1 | Type of plant | Cost of pot (£) | Cost of compost (£) | Weeks to reach full size | Weekly cost of keeping plant | Total cost of plant | Selling price of plant | Number of plants sold | Total profit |
| 2 | Rose | 0.30 | 0.15 | 16 | 0.05 | 1.25 | 1.88 | 150 | 93.75 |
| 3 | Pear tree | 0.70 | 0.75 | 52 | 0.05 | 4.05 | 6.08 | 75 | 151.88 |
| 4 | Pansy | 0.02 | 0.02 | 4 | 0.08 | 0.36 | 0.54 | 325 | 58.50 |
| 5 | Lavender | 0.08 | 0.10 | 12 | 0.04 | 0.66 | 0.99 | 125 | 41.25 |
| 6 | Holly | 0.15 | 0.20 | 16 | 0.04 | 0.99 | 1.49 | 147 | 72.77 |
| 7 |  |  |  |  |  |  |  | Total profit | 418.15 |

**a** Shade in the cell which shows the cost of compost for a lavender plant.

**b** The formula used to work out the selling price in cell G3 is

=F3*1.5

Write down the formula which is needed in each of the cells below.

   **i**  I7
   **ii**  F3

**c  i**  Which cell would you change to find the effect on the profit of selling more Pear trees?

   **ii**  Which cells would change as a result?            (NEAB)

**2** A spreadsheet is used to work out the cost of producing a toy dog. Part of the spreadsheet is shown below.

|  | A | B | C | D | E | F |
|---|---|---|---|---|---|---|
| 1 2 | Item | Cost for 1 pack (£) | Number in pack | Cost for 1 item (£) | Number needed for 1 dog | Cost of items for 1 dog (£) |
| 3 | eyes | 0.25 | 50 |  | 2 |  |
| 4 | nose | 0.75 | 50 |  | 1 |  |
| 5 | collar | 0.75 | 10 |  | 1 |  |
| 6 | lead | 0.90 | 10 |  | 1 |  |
| 7 | body | 5.50 | 5 |  | 1 |  |
| 8 | legs | 1.00 | 12 |  | 4 |  |
| 9 |  |  |  |  | Total cost for 1 dog |  |
| 10 |  |  |  |  |  |  |
| 11 |  |  |  |  |  |  |

**a** Write down the formula needed in the cells given below.
   **i**  D3
   **ii**  F3
   **iii**  F9

**b** A profit of half the cost of making a dog is required. How could the spreadsheet be extended so that it works out the selling price of the dog?

**c** Give four advantages of using a spreadsheet to work out the cost of a dog rather than using a calculator.     (NEAB)

**3** Concrete Products Ltd are a small company which produce items of garden furniture. They use a spreadsheet like the one here to help them in their business.

Data is contained in cells. Each cell is given an address, which is a letter followed by a number. For example the cell with the address A8 contains the word Heron.

|    | A | B | C | D | E | F | G | H |
|----|---|---|---|---|---|---|---|---|
| 1 | Type of | Cost of | Cost of | Total | Desired | Selling | Number | Potential |
| 2 | furniture | materials | Labour | cost | profit for 1 | price each | made this week | profit this week |
| 3 | Bird bath | 11.50 | 11.00 | 22.50 | 2.50 | 25.00 | 45 | 112.50 |
| 4 | Gnome | 5.50 | 8.00 | 13.50 | 1.50 | 15.00 | 120 | 180.00 |
| 5 | Frog | 5.00 | 5.00 | 10.00 | 2.00 | 12.00 | 90 | 180.00 |
| 6 | Sundial | 22.00 | 12.00 | 34.00 | 3.00 | 37.00 | 55 | 165.00 |
| 7 | Toadstool | 4.50 | 6.00 | 10.50 | 3.00 | 13.50 | 125 | 375.00 |
| 8 | Heron | 8.50 | 6.00 | 14.50 | 3.00 | 17.50 | 80 | 240.00 |
| 9 | Plant tub | 7.00 | 5.00 | 12.00 | 2.00 | 14.00 | 100 | 200.00 |
| 10 | | | | | | | | |
| 11 | | | | | | | Total profit | 1452.50 |

a The cost of materials needed to make a heron increases to £10.00.
  
  i Give the address of the cell that you would have to change on the spreadsheet.
  
  ii After this was changed the numbers in cells D8 and H8 would change. Give the addresses of two other cells in which the numbers would also change.
  
  iii The numbers in the cells change because the cell contains a formula.
  
  Write the formula which would be in cell D8
  Write the formula which would be in cell H8

b Concrete Products Ltd has decided to investigate the effect of calculating the profit rather than using a fixed amount. The profit will be one quarter of the costs involved in making an item.
  
  i Which column would you have to change?
  
  ii What formula would you have to enter into row 3 of this column?                                    (NEAB

4 Home Furniture Ltd is a business which makes a small range of wooden furniture for the home. They have created a spreadsheet like this one to help them calculate the cost of making each item.

Data is contained in cells. Each cell is given an address, which is a letter followed by a number. For example, the cell with the address A5 contains the text **Video Cabinet**.

a What is the address of the cell which shows the cost of materials needed to make one office desk?

|  | A | B | C | D | E | F | G | H |
|---|---|---|---|---|---|---|---|---|
| 1 | Item of | Cost of | Time taken to | Pay per | Total Pay | Total cost | Number made | Total weekly |
| 2 | furniture | Materials (£) | make 1 unit (hrs) | hours (£) | for 1 unit (£) | for 1 unit (£) | each week | cost (£) |
| 3 | Bookcase | 32.00 | 3 | 2.50 | 7.50 | 39.50 | 60 | 2370.00 |
| 4 | Bedside Cabinet | 26.00 | 2 | 2.50 | 5.00 | 31.00 | 100 | 3100.00 |
| 5 | Video Cabinet | 35.00 | 4 | 3.50 | 14.00 | 49.00 | 80 | 3920.00 |
| 6 | HiFi Cabinet | 37.00 | 4 | 3.50 | 14.00 | 51.00 | 80 | 4080.00 |
| 7 | Computer Desk | 40.00 | 3 | 3.00 | 9.00 | 49.00 | 120 | 5880.00 |
| 8 | Office Desk | 36.00 | 3 | 3.00 | 9.00 | 45.00 | 100 | 4500.00 |
| 9 |  |  |  |  |  |  |  |  |
| 10 |  |  |  |  |  | Grand total | weekly cost (£) | 23850.00 |

b Place a tick next to the statement which is used to work out the values in the column **Total pay for 1 unit**.

| Cost of Materials × Pay per hour |  |
|---|---|
| Time taken to make 1 unit × Total cost for 1 unit |  |
| Cost of Materials × Time taken to make 1 unit |  |
| Time taken to make 1 unit × Pay per hour |  |
| Cost of Materials + Time taken to make 1 unit |  |

c The number of hours it takes to make one computer desk was entered incorrectly. It should be 4 hours.
  i Give the address of the cell that you would have to change on the spreadsheet.
  ii After this was changed, the numbers in cells F7 and H7 would change. Give the addresses of **two other** cells which would also change as a result.

d The numbers in the cells change because the cell contains a formula.
  From the list below, choose the correct formula which would be in cell:
  =F7*G7    =B7*E7    =B7+E7
  =F7+G7    =B7+G7    =B7*G7
  i F7
  ii H7

e It has been decided that all workers who make the furniture will now get the same rate of pay, which will be £4.50. Column D (Pay per hour) can now be removed from the spreadsheet.
  Write down the formula which would have to be entered in row 3 of the **Total pay for 1 unit** column in order to calculate the total pay to make one bookcase if column D was removed from the spreadsheet.                    (NEAB)

# Simulation software

Modelling using spreadsheets has many limitations – it can't respond quickly to rapidly changing inputs and its output is limited to a table of numbers containing the answer, or a graph or a chart. To simulate situations realistically the model needs to respond rapidly to inputs and the output might include changing graphics, and possibly also movement and sound. The computer program used to set up this kind of model is much more complex than a spreadsheet.

## ■ *Flight simulators*

A full-scale flight simulator of the type used to train pilots (you can see one of these in the photographs) provides a graphics display of what is visible from the plane. The 'plane' the pilot sits in is moved by motors and the dials and displays showing the position and condition of the 'plane' are updated by the computer in response to the actions the trainee pilot takes to adjust the controls. Sensors detect the pilot's adjustments and this input data is used to control the graphics display, the system that moves the 'cabin' and the readouts on the control panel. The conditions of 'flight' and 'landing' can be changed for different circumstances – for example different airports and different weather conditions – so the pilot can learn to fly without any danger.

*A flight simulator doesn't look much like a plane!*

*What the inside of a flight simulator looks like*

The whole system is very complex but gives a quite realistic effect. The system collects data every time the **simulation** is run and can produce printouts to show exactly what the pilot did at each stage in the 'flight'. Even though the computer program controlling the simulator is very complex, this kind of model, like the simpler spreadsheet model, still relies on rules built into the program – the rules in a simulator are just a lot more complex than spreadsheet formulae. The simulator also produces a **real-time response** – the output is adjusted in immediate response to the input data.

A training system like this is much safer to use than learning in a real plane. It can be used to simulate emergency situations (such as engine failure or fire) and give the pilot practice in handling a dangerous situation which *might* never occur but which would require a correct and rapid response if it did happen.

# ■ *Other simulations*

Car designers use simulators to test the aerodynamic effects of changes in the shape of cars. The car's shape is designed on computer using a CAD package, and the output is a mathematical description of the shape. The effects of this shape on the flow of air over it are worked out by the simulation program rather than by actually building a car body and putting it in a wind tunnel. This saves time and money and lets the designers work out how relatively small changes in the shape will affect the air flow by repeating tests – the shape can be changed and the test repeated until the designers are happy with the results.

Can you think of any other situations where simulators are used?

*A real wind tunnel*

*A simulation of a wind tunnel*

**Q**

**Why is a spreadsheet model no good for a realistic simulation like a flight simulator?**

**What are the benefits of using a flight simulator rather than using a real plane? Are there any disadvantages?**

**The quality of a simulation depends on a number of factors – what are they?**

# Limitations of simulators

Whatever type of simulation or model is used it is very important to remember that the simulation is *not* the real world. A simulator can't *prove* what will actually happen – the model may be wrong in some way.

- Even a fairly simple model can have quite a lot of rules – if one of these is not always true then the results will be wrong for some situations.
- Variables that can affect the outcome might not have been taken into account in constructing the model.
- Many processes and situations can be influenced by random events like fire and bad weather conditions, so when we construct a model we must try to work out what could have an effect – even if it's unlikely.
- The data used in constructing the model is very important – if we put in wrong data values then the answers we get will be wrong.

# Summary

- Programs that produce realistic simulations are more complex than spreadsheet models.
- The simulation system often includes input from sensors of some kind.
- Outputs often include graphics and may include control signals to motors designed to bring about movement.
- In systems of this type, data is often collected to be analysed later.
- No matter how complex a simulation is, it is not reality and is only as good as the rules it's based on.

## Questions

1 Explain why a simulator might be used for the following:

   a Training pilots
   b Investigating the effect of a river barrage scheme
   c Trying out safety systems in a new power station design
   d Designing a better shape for the body of a car

2 A flight simulator is developed as a computer game. Why would certain aspects of the control of the aircraft be omitted from the simulation? (MEG)

3 Write down **two** reasons why some situations are modelled using a computer. (MEG)

4 Motor manufacturers are now fitting air bags as safety features on many new cars.
   They use computer simulations to test how these air bags work in different crash conditions.

   a Give **two** reasons why computer simulations are used **in this situation**.
   b After these simulations have been carried out, the air bags are tested in crash situations using real cars. Why is this necessary? (NEAB)

5 Computer models are used in a wide variety of situations, such as training pilots and simulating a leak in a nuclear reactor?

   i What is a computer model?
   ii Give **three** reasons for using computer models. (NEAB)

# Measurement and Control

## ■ *What is control?*

Control is making things work as you want them to. A computer program can control movement. It can control the movement of a robot connected to it, opening of doors in a high security area or the movement of a screen image. If the device it is controlling is outside the computer, rather than an image on screen, then it will be connected to the computer through an **interface unit** that converts the data from the computer into signals which operate the device.

### CONTROLLING AN IMAGE ON SCREEN

Let's start by thinking about how the computer controls a screen image. The computer can't move something on the screen by itself – it needs instructions telling it what to do. These instructions have to be given to the computer in a **programming language**. One language that is often used for control programs is called **LOGO**. Using instructions in LOGO a computer can be used to control a symbol called a 'turtle' on the screen, or a robot turtle on the floor (like the one in the photograph). LOGO has commands to make the turtle go forwards, backwards, left, right, stop and lift a pen up or put the pen down. A robot turtle has a real pen to draw shapes on sheets of paper on the floor – a screen 'turtle' draws a line on the screen as it moves. 'Pendown' makes the turtle draw, 'penup' stops it drawing. The 'home' instruction sends the turtle to the middle of the screen, pointing upwards.

You can use the turtle to draw pictures on the screen and to help you learn about control programs.

Most of the instructions in LOGO include a number.

> *FORWARD 50 tells the computer to move the robot forward 50 'turtle steps'.*

> *LEFT 90 tells the computer to turn the robot left through 90°.*

*A robot turtle.*

You can type the instructions in one at a time and the computer will carry out each instruction and wait for the next. This method will work, but you can't save your work and if you need to start again you'll have to start from the beginning. A much better method is to put the instructions together to make a program. A **program** is a series of instructions in the correct order that make the computer carry out a particular task.

LOGO programs are made up of procedures. A **procedure** is a group of instructions, with a name. In Figure 12.1 you can see a program to make the screen turtle draw a simple shape.

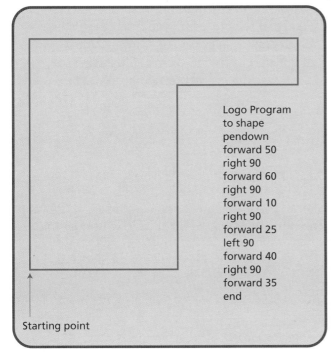

```
Logo Program
to shape
pendown
forward 50
right 90
forward 60
right 90
forward 10
right 90
forward 25
left 90
forward 40
right 90
forward 35
end
```

Starting point

**Figure 12.1** *The program to make a robot turtle draw a shape*

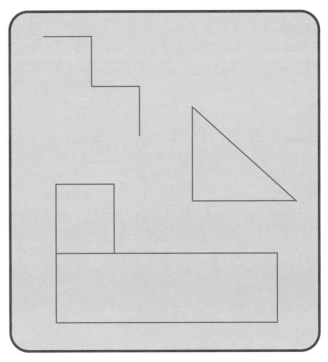

**Figure 12.2** *Shapes to draw using LOGO*

Look at the shapes in Figure 12.2 and try writing a LOGO program to draw them. You can use these instructions:

> *forward*
> *right*
> *left*
> *back*
> *penup*
> *pendown*

**Figure 12.3** *A rather complicated looking picture, that is really prepared using only squares of the same size*

**Figure 12.4** *Different sized squares can be drawn on the same picture if you use the right procedure*

Don't forget, if you want the computer to move the turtle you must tell it how far you want it to go. If you are telling the computer to turn the turtle you have to let it know how many degrees to turn through.

When we want to produce more complex movement or shapes, we often need to repeat the same instructions several times. LOGO gives us an easy way to do this – a repeating **loop** in the program. For example, to make a square with sides 40 'turtle steps' long, you can use this procedure:

> *to square*
> *repeat 4 [forward 40 right 90]*
> *end*

(The computer will repeat the instructions in the square brackets four times). Once you have typed in the procedure you can use the name 'square' as an instruction to draw as many squares as you want.

Figure 12.3 is a picture made entirely of squares all the same size. These squares were drawn using the instructions in this procedure:

> *to flower*
> *repeat 36 [square left 10]*
> *end*

This time there are two instructions in the brackets, which are repeated 36 times.

We don't always want to make a picture of shapes that are all the same size. If we alter the procedure called square we can allow for this. The new version is:

> *to square :side*
> *repeat 4 [forward: side right 90]*
> *end*

All you need to do to make squares of whatever size you want, in whatever position, is to write a new procedure to move the turtle to the starting point you want for each square, and provide the side length for the square procedure (this was done to give the picture in Figure 12.4).

The flower patterns in Figure 12.5 were drawn using this procedure, which we called 'pattern':

> *to pattern*
> *home*
> *pen up*
> *back 100*
> *pen down*
> *repeat 36 [square 40 left 10]*
> *pen up*
> *left 10*
> *forward 120*
> *pen down*

*repeat 36 [square 30 left 10]*
*pen up*
*left 10*
*back 40*
*right 90*
*forward 70*
*left 90*
*pen down*
*repeat 36 [square 20 left 10]*
*pen up*
*left 100*
*forward 140*
*right 90*
*pen down*
*repeat 36 [square 20 left 10]*
*end*

**Q**

**What is the triangular screen image used with programs like LOGO often called?**

**Explain what is meant by**

    **Program**
    **Procedure**
    **Interface unit**

Now, when we type 'pattern', the computer moves the turtle and draws a flower pattern. The movements given to the computer must be exact or we won't get proper flower shapes in the pattern we want. Read the instructions carefully and work out how the turtle is moving.

Now write some LOGO programs of your own to make repeating patterns.

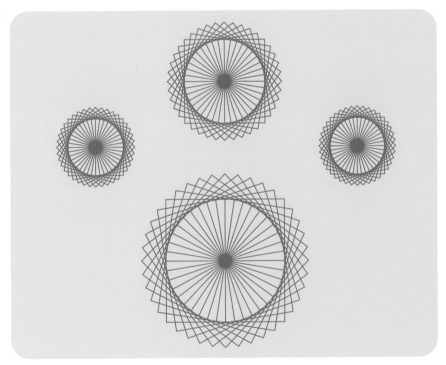

**Figure 12.5** *A pattern of four flower shapes drawn using LOGO*

# Using the computer to measure changes

Computers can be used to measure changes in conditions such as temperature and amount of light (you might want to record changes in weather conditions outside your school, for example). Suitable sensors have to be attached to the computer system for it to be able to make these measurements. The sensors are attached through an interface unit or **buffer box**. A buffer box has sockets to plug in the sensors, and converts the continuously varying (**analogue**) signal from the sensor into a **digital** signal which the computer can use.

# Sensors

Different kinds of sensors can be used to detect different things – like heat, light, touch (pressure) and infrared.

Before the readings from the sensor can be used, you must **calibrate** the sensor by matching particular sensor readings with known values in the units required. Once two readings have been matched the computer can calculate all the rest. For example, if you put a heat sensor in ice at 0°C and store this reading, then put it in boiling water at 100°C and store this reading, the computer will be able to work out the temperature for all the other readings between 0°C and 100°C.

# Choosing the right sensor

You must be very careful to choose the right sensor for what you are going to measure. Different heat sensors work over different ranges of temperature and provide different levels of accuracy. You wouldn't use the same sensor to detect small changes in room temperature and to detect temperature changes in a central heating boiler, though you would find both kinds in a central heating control system in your home or at school.

When you are designing a system that will use sensors you need to consider these factors:

- What you are measuring.
- What range of values you expect to read.
- How the sensors will be positioned.
- How they will be protected – if you want to use a sensor to measure air temperature you will have to protect it from direct sunlight or you won't get an accurate reading (why?).

# Using data from sensors

The computer program can use the data collected from sensors to make the decisions needed to control a device accurately. For example, the data from sensors on the arm of a robot can be used to control the movement of the robot properly. Using data from sensors to control output signals like this is called **feedback**.

Sensors on the claws of a robot's 'hand' can detect the pressure which builds up as it grips an object and the computer can be programmed to switch off the claw motor when the pressure is just strong enough to grip the object but not so strong that the object gets crushed. The robot in the photograph seems to have got it just right!

Sensors are sometimes just used to collect data for use later, and the data collected is stored in files on disk. This is called **data-logging**. The computer can be programmed to store data over a certain time and the time interval between each measurement, called the **sampling interval**, can also be set.

*This robot's hand has to be very carefully controlled to be able to hold this egg without breaking it.*

## MELTING ICE

If we want to investigate the way temperature changes as ice melts we can use a heat sensor calibrated so that the computer gives readings in °C. The sensor doesn't need to operate over a very wide range of temperatures but it *does* have to be able to detect very small temperature changes. The sensor we choose will need to be mounted in a waterproof casing so that when it is placed in the melting ice it isn't damaged by the water.

Once the apparatus is set up (as shown in the photograph), with the sensor surrounded by crushed ice in the beaker, we need to collect our data. At this stage we don't know exactly what will happen to the temperature or how long it will take to finish the experiment. We can start by collecting data over a period of about an hour and can collect data every 30 seconds or every minute (if we collect data more often than this we will use up a lot of disk space). If, during this first investigation, we find that the changes between each reading are very large, then we can stop the experiment and try again with a shorter sampling interval. If we used sampling intervals of 5 minutes we might not have enough data to be sure that no more changes had happened at the point where all the ice had melted.

Once we have collected the data we can use it to plot graphs or the data can be transferred into a spreadsheet package to be used in calculations. Figure 12.6 is a graph produced from data collected in an experiment like this.

We could keep the computer and the sensor close together in this experiment but this isn't possible for some data-logging applications. For example, when weather forecasters collect data about weather conditions in remote areas the sensors have to transmit the data to the computer over long distances, which often involves satellite systems.

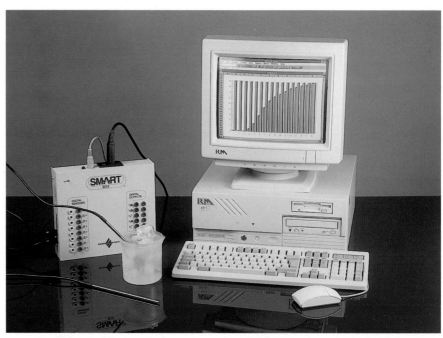

*Experimental set-up for sensing the temperature in melting ice*

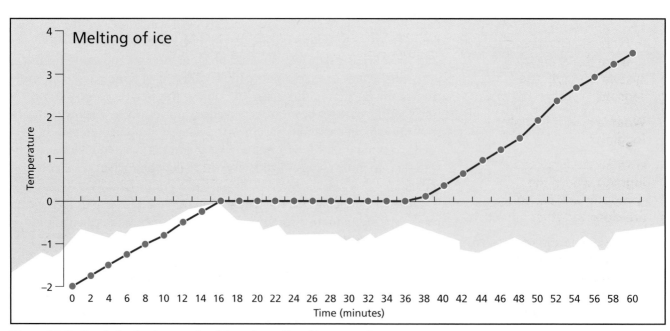

**Figure 12.6** *Graph that has been produced from data collected in an experiment*

*A weather balloon sends its data back to the ground by telemetry*

Data about atmospheric conditions can be collected by attaching the sensing equipment to a weather balloon (you can see one in the photograph) which rises through the air. As it does so it transmits data about the altitude and weather conditions back to the computer on the ground. This sort of data transmission is called **telemetry**.

# Constructing a device that responds to data from sensors

To learn about feedback and how devices can be made to respond to data collected by sensors you can make a model. Your model will have devices for the computer to control, and sensors to collect data.

> *For safety and legal reasons you must not try to control mains-powered equipment. Use batteries or a low-voltage power supply.*

**Q**

**Name four different kinds of things which sensors can detect**

**Describe the process of calibration**

**List three details you need to consider when you are designing a system that will use sensors**

**What is meant by data-logging?**

**Give an example of data-logging where the computer and sensor(s) are close together**

**Give an example of data-logging in which the data from the sensor(s) would have to be transmitted over long distances**

## A MODEL GREENHOUSE CONTROL SYSTEM

In this section we are going to build a model of a greenhouse. The computer must keep the temperature above 18°C, turn the light on when it gets dark, turn the heater off if the temperature gets above 22°C and turn the light off when there is normal daylight in the greenhouse.

The model greenhouse control system is an example of the use of feedback – data from a sensor is used to control a device which can alter the conditions the sensor detects. Figure 12.7 shows how feedback works in this system.

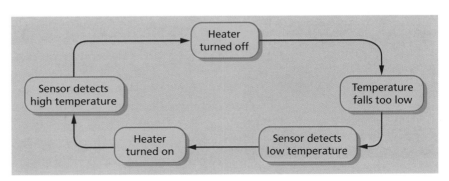

**Figure 12.7** *How feedback works in a greenhouse control system.*

## STEP 1: DESIGN THE GREENHOUSE MODEL

It needs to be transparent so light can get in. You will need room for the sensors, the light and the heater. You will probably want to build your model, but you don't need to put plants inside. Remember, this is just a model so it can be quite small and simple – a big clear jar would probably do.

## STEP 2: DECIDE ON THE SENSORS YOU WILL USE AND WHERE YOU NEED TO PLACE THEM

You need to think about the range of temperatures that will probably be measured and choose the right kind of heat sensor. You will also need a light sensor that can operate over a very wide range of light conditions, from very dark to bright sunlight.

## STEP 3: DECIDE ON WHAT DEVICES YOU WILL NEED TO KEEP THE GREENHOUSE CONDITIONS JUST RIGHT

In this model you need to control a light and a heater. The model isn't very big so choose ones with low power ratings.

## STEP 4: PUT THE SENSORS AND DEVICES IN PLACE AND CONNECT THEM TO THE COMPUTER THROUGH THE INTERFACE UNIT

Be very careful when you're placing the sensors. Don't get them too close to the devices they work with or you won't get good results. If the heat sensor is directly above the heater then the sensor will get warm before the rest of your model greenhouse warms up. Why shouldn't you let light from your light bulb hit the light sensor?

## STEP 5: DESIGN AND WRITE A PROGRAM TO READ THE SENSOR DATA AND TURN THE DEVICES ON AND OFF AS NEEDED

You must be careful about how far you let the temperature change before switching the heater on or off. If you use very narrow temperature limits you'll end up switching the heater on and off very frequently – maybe several times a second – and this level of control isn't necessary in a greenhouse. You also need to program the computer to turn the light on when it gets dark and off when it gets light, but you don't want it flashing

*You could use a kit like this to build your model greenhouse*

on and off. In a real greenhouse flashing lights would disturb the people working with the plants.

Designing a program needs special care. You have to decide what the program must be able to do and produce a plan (called an **algorithm**) to show how you will make the program do this, stage by stage. The best way to prepare your design is to work out the main stages first then write down the steps needed to make each stage happen. Remember – you're designing a program for the computer, not actions for you to carry out.

### Main stages

These are the main stages you'll need to think about:

1 Calibrate sensors
2 Set allowed ranges for light and temperature
3 Set interval for checking sensors
4 Check sensors and if necessary adjust heater and light (repeat this stage continuously).

Now, looking at each stage in more detail, let's decide what steps each stage requires.

### Stage 1

- Read heat sensor at known temperature 1
- Store temperature 1
- Read heat sensor at known temperature 2
- Store temperature 2
- Calibrate heat sensor
- Read light sensor in bright daylight
- Store light intensity 1
- Read light sensor in dark
- Store light intensity 2
- Calibrate light sensor.

### Stage 2

- Store maximum temperature allowed
- Store minimum temperature allowed
- Store maximum light allowed
- Store minimum light allowed.

### Stage 3

- Store time interval to use between each set of sensor readings.

### Stage 4

Repeat these steps until the computer is switched off:
- Read heat sensor
- If temperature is below the minimum allowed then turn heater on
- If temperature is above the maximum allowed then turn heater off

- If light is less than the minimum allowed then turn light on
- If light is more than or equal to the maximum allowed then turn light off
- Wait for time interval.

You can easily convert this plan into a computer program in a suitable language like Control LOGO or BASIC.

## STEP 6: TEST YOUR GREENHOUSE CONTROL SYSTEM TO CHECK THAT IT WORKS

You need to check that the light goes on when it is dark. Cover up the model or put it in a box to do this test.

Check that the temperature stays within the limits you have set. You can do this by putting a thermometer inside the model and reading the temperature frequently. You could try cooling your model down by putting it next to an open window or in a fridge.

## OTHER CONTROL SYSTEMS

The greenhouse control system we've just described is just one example of using feedback. Similar systems are used to control the conditions inside large buildings or to control manufacturing processes, for example producing sheets of metal of required thickness. Can you think of any others?

# Summary

- A computer is capable of controlling an external device or an image on the screen when it is programmed in an appropriate way.
- Controlling a device needs a program to tell the computer what to do.
- The instructions you give the computer must be accurate or it won't control the device as you expect it to.
- Computers can be used to collect data using sensors. This is called data-logging.
- Different sensors detect different things, over different ranges and to different degrees of accuracy.
- The intervals between reading the sensor values must be suitable for the investigation being carried out. Sometimes you need to try a few different intervals to find which works best.

- The time over which data is collected must be suitable for the investigation being carried out.
- Data can be collected using sensors a long way from the computer.
- The data collected can be saved on disk for analysis in other software packages.
- When you design a system in which a device responds to data that has been collected it is important to think about the type of sensor, where it is placed, what protection it needs and the program that collects the data and controls the device.

# ■ *Suggestions for control and measurement work*

- Write programs in LOGO to draw shapes or control a turtle.
- Set up a computer system to compare the variation in temperature in a room and the variation in the temperature outside, saving the data so you can analyse it later.

## INVESTIGATIONS

Using a computer, interface unit and software,

- investigate the movement of a trolley along a ramp
- measure temperature changes during a chemical reaction
- measure the heat given off by decomposing leaves
- construct a model of a burglar alarm system
- construct a model of a car park barrier
- use data from sensors to monitor the temperature of a fish tank and sound an alarm if it gets too hot or too cold.

# Questions

**1** A floor turtle can use the following instructions.

| INSTRUCTION | DESCRIPTION |
|---|---|
| FORWARD $n$ | Move $n$ cm forward |
| BACKWARD $n$ | Move $n$ cm backward |
| LEFT $t$ | Turn left $t$ degrees |
| RIGHT $t$ | Turn right $t$ degrees |
| PEN UP | Lift the pen off the paper |
| PEN DOWN | Place the pen on the paper |

Write a set of instructions which make the turtle draw the following shape.

**2** A floor turtle can use the following instructions.

| | |
|---|---|
| FORWARD $n$ | Move $n$ cm forward |
| BACKWARD $n$ | Move $n$ cm backward |
| LEFT $t$ | Turn left $t$ degrees |
| RIGHT $t$ | Turn right $t$ degrees |
| PEN UP | Lift the pen off the paper |
| PEN DOWN | Place the pen on the paper |

Write a set of instructions which makes the turtle draw a rectangle of sides 30 cm by 50 cm.

**3** A computer system controls a robot turtle. The turtle holds a pen. When the turtle moves, the pen leaves a line on the paper beneath it.

The turtle is moved by typing commands into the computer system.

The commands which are used to move the turtle are as follows:

FORWARD distance                    (in cm)

LEFT angle                          (in degrees)

RIGHT angle                         (in degrees)

so FORWARD 20 would move the turtle forward 20 cm

and LEFT 45 would turn the turtle left through an angle of 45 degrees.

**a** Using only the commands in the list below, write down the set of instructions needed to draw this shape.

**Command List**

**FORWARD 30**

**FORWARD 50**

**FORWARD 70**

**LEFT 90**

**RIGHT 90**

You may need to use some of the commands in the list more than once.

**b** Write down the instructions needed for the following shape.
You must still only use the commands FORWARD, RIGHT and LEFT, but with any distance and angles you may need.

(NEAB)

**5** A computer system can control an arrow on a screen. When the arrow moves forward, it leaves a line.
The arrow is moved by typing commands into the computer system.
The commands which are used to move the arrow are as follows:
FORWARD distance
LEFT angle
RIGHT angle

so FORWARD 30 would move the arrow forward 30 units and RIGHT 90 would turn the arrow through an angle of 90 degrees.

a Using only the commands in the list below, write down the set of instructions needed to draw this shape:

**Command List**
**FORWARD 20**
**FORWARD 30**
**FORWARD 75**
**LEFT 90**
**RIGHT 90**

You may need to use some of the commands in the list more than once.

b Write down the instructions needed for the following shape.
You must still only use the commands FORWARD, RIGHT and LEFT, but with any distance and angles you may need.

6 Fill in the gaps in the paragraph below using words from the following list.

| | | |
|---|---|---|
| switch | light | siren |
| motor | controlled | validated |
| heat | feedback | computers |
| pressure | sensors | detect |
| switched | keypads | cards |

A building is protected by a computer .................... security system.

.................... are placed at various points in the building to .................... what is happening.

When it gets dark the outside of the building is lit up by floodlights. A .................... sensor provides the data needed to operate these.

Underneath the carpet near the doors are ....................
sensors. If someone breaks in a .................... sounds.   (NEAB)

9 A floor robot is travelling through an obstacle course. Name **two** sensors which can be used to detect an obstacle.

(MEG)

**10** Describe **three** types of sensor used in burglar alarms to detect entry into a house. (MEG)

**11** A floor robot is placed at the entrance to a maze. It travels through the maze, eventually reaching the exit having made many wrong turns. The second time through the maze it travels directly to the exit without making a mistake.
Describe the features of the robot which enable it to do this. (MEG)

**12** To help increase security at their home, Mr. and Mrs. Patel have decided to fit a light to the outside of their house. They want the light to come on when a person approaches the house and it is dark.
Light sensors will be fitted to detect when it is dark.

   **a** Give **two different** types of sensor that could be fitted to detect when a person approaches.
   **b** Explain why more than one light sensor may be needed.
   **c** Explain why the sensors may need to be calibrated to a known scale before use. (NEAB)

**13** Computers can be used in science laboratories to collect data from experiments.

   **a** Give **three** reasons why computers are used in this way.
   **b** Give **one** example of an experiment in which data-logging is used.
   **c** Describe how Information Technology is used to create a report on the experiment. (MEG)

**14** A computer system is to be set up in a school laboratory.

   **a** Identify **two** safety issues which must be considered.
   **b** Describe **two** sensors which could be attached to the computer to collect data from experiments. (MEG)

**15 a** Give **one** situation in which a data-logging device is used.
**b** Why is a data logger used in this situation? (MEG)

**16** Fill in the gaps in the paragraph below using words from the following list.

| | | |
|---|---|---|
| graph | monitor | minute |
| disc drive | collection | fixed |
| sensors | period | cards |
| day | frequency | computer |
| storage | validation | hour |

Data logging is the .................... and .................... of data from sensors. Data is obtained at .................... intervals over a given .................... of time. The sensors can be connected directly to a .................... for processing or data can be stored off-line. This processing could be the production of a .................... or a table. (NEAB)

**17** Sensors can be attached to a computer system and used to collect data.

In a geography investigation, students are studying how temperature varies during the course of 24 hours. A sensor is connected to a computer to take readings.

**a** What do we call this method of data capture?
**b i** What kind of sensor should be used?
  **ii** Why is this sensor needed?
**c i** How often should a reading be taken?
  **ii** Why is this a suitable interval?
**d** How could this data be presented in a report on the investigation? (NEAB)

**18** Sensors attached to a computer system can be used to collect data at regular intervals.

**a** What do we call this method of collecting data?
**b** A pupil decides to use sensors attached to a computer system to collect data about how hot tea cools in different shaped cups.
  **i** What kind of sensor should the pupil use?
  **ii** How often should the pupil collect data? Choose the **best** time interval and write the letter in the box.
    **A** Every tenth of a second
    **B** Every minute
    **C** Every 20 minutes
    **D** Every hour
  **iii** For how long should the pupil collect data? Choose the **best** time interval and write the letter in the box.
    **A** For 1 second

**B** For 1 minute
**C** For 5 minutes
**D** For 1 hour
**E** For 12 hours

19 A computer system is used to control the temperature of a large warehouse.
The system consists of a computer connected to three separate temperature sensors and a heater.

a Give **two** reasons why three sensors are used in this system.
b The temperature must be kept above 20°C but no extra heat is needed when the temperature reaches 25°C. Explain how the control program would keep the temperature correct. (NEAB)

20 A company breeds large numbers of fish for fish farms. The young fish will only grow if they have enough oxygen. A computer system is used to control the amount of oxygen in the tanks. Sensors in the tanks detect the amount of oxygen in the water. A pump connected to the computer system can be used to pump oxygen into the tanks.
Explain how **monitoring and feedback** can be used to make sure the fish have enough oxygen. (NEAB)

21 Feedback is used when implementing a system including monitoring and control.

a What is meant by **feedback** in the above sentence?
b i Give **one** example of a monitoring and control system which uses feedback.
ii Briefly describe how feedback is used in this system. (NEAB)

# Evaluating Software Packages

You'll often find that you need to choose from several software packages of the same type when you're solving a particular IT problem – you might have two or three different spreadsheet packages available, more than one database package, and two or three different word processing packages.

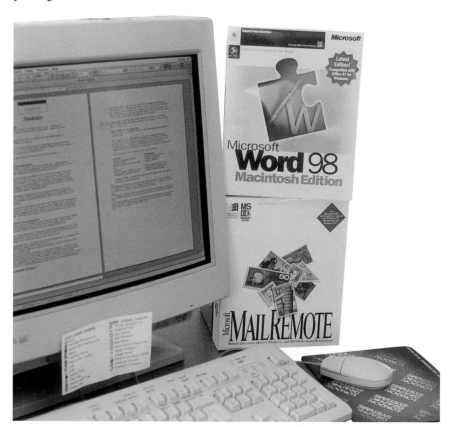

*Word processing packages*

Choosing which *kind* of package you need to use is nearly always quite straightforward, but deciding *which* package of that type will do the job best is not quite so easy.

You can't make reasoned decisions unless you **evaluate** each of the packages available. Evaluating a package means finding out how well it does the kind of job you want it to do. You can't do this without having a list of tasks the package must carry out.

For example, if you want to produce a report of a science experiment you might need to use a package which can:

- handle ordinary text
- handle special characters, for example letters from the Greek alphabet ($\alpha$, $\beta$, $\gamma$)
- produce subscripts, for example the number 2 in the formula $H_2O$
- produce superscripts – for example the 3 in $cm^3$
- produce neat tables with numbers and headings lined up properly
- import charts from a spreadsheet
- import drawings from a drawing package
- allow large files for long reports
- number the pages
- be easy to use with help available on screen when needed.

You will need to find out if the word-processing package can do these things, and also how easily it does them.

To carry out an evaluation, make a complete list of everything you need the package to do. Put these in order of importance because sometimes you will have to settle for the best package available when none of them do everything you would like. Remember, how easy the package is to use is very important, especially if you are producing a system to be used by other, inexperienced users.

Once your list is complete, work through all the tasks for one package, and give the package a score for each item (you might give 5 points if it does the job well, 4 if there are one or two minor difficulties, 3 if it is quite hard to learn to carry out a task, 2 if the task takes far too long and is difficult to carry out, 1 if it can only be done with extreme difficulty, so that you would probably avoid doing it at all and 0 if it doesn't do the task at all). Be consistent in you scoring. When you have done this for all your packages you will be able to make a reasoned judgement about which package is best.

If you're asked to recommend a package to someone else, you shouldn't just give them your scores because they might not mean much to someone else. You should produce an evaluation report, explaining what tasks you have tried, what you have found out, and include some printouts of what the packages can do. At the end of your report you should describe the strengths and weaknesses you have found and make your recommendation.

## Questions

1 Middlebridge School has installed a computer system to help run the school. Data about pupils is stored on a database.
  a User documentation is required to help the staff at the school use the system.
    i  One section of this documentation deals with 'normal working procedures'.
      State **four** items which would be covered in this section.
    ii State **three** other sections which may be contained in the user documentation for the system.      (NEAB)

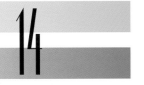

# Producing and Documenting Systems

If you have worked through this book you will already have designed some systems that use IT to solve specific problems. You will probably have written down something about the systems you have produced, but you probably won't have fully **documented** your systems. **Documentation** is the written material (the **document**) that explains how a system works and how to use it. Producing good, clear documentation is as important as designing a good, efficient system. If the people who want to use your system can't understand the instructions you've written then the whole system is a failure.

When you're producing a system for others to use it is vital that it works as efficiently as possible, so the user can get what they want out of it as quickly and easily as possible.

## ◼ *Producing the system specification*

It is very important to find out everything that the user needs the system to do, but finding this out isn't always easy! Your user might not know much about IT so you might need to make helpful suggestions. When users describe what they want from a system, they often miss out important tasks, perhaps because they don't happen very often. You will have to talk to the people who will use your system and make notes about what they say they want the system to do. If your system is intended to replace an existing way of doing the job, you will find that watching what happens at present will help you make sure nothing gets left out. You will also need to check for any **constraints** on the system you produce – your user might need a system that works on a particular make of computer, or can only afford to pay a certain amount for the final system.

When you have collected all this information you can write a **system specification**. The system specification says what the system must be able to do. It may also:

- include information on the number of records or amount of data the system must be able to handle and store

- say how quickly the output must be produced
- specify the computer system to be used
- give a date when the system must be complete and ready for use.

The system specification needs to be quite detailed as it will be used to decide whether the final system performs as it should. A successful system meets all the requirements in the system specification.

## Producing a school newsletter

To make the process clear, let's look at how we could create a system to produce a school newsletter. The newsletter will be issued free to all pupils every two weeks. It is to be produced by a group of pupils and staff and duplicated in the school office.

Here is the specification for the system:

1 The system must be capable of including line drawings, photographs and text.
2 The newsletter will be printed in black on coloured paper.
3 A standard heading will be used for all issues.
4 Pages will always be divided into two columns.
5 Apart from the front page, all pages will have the same layout.
6 Articles and news items will be collected from pupils and staff and most will be hand-written.
7 The newsletter must be put together within two days of collecting all the news items.
8 It must be possible to alter what is on the pages after the first copy is printed and before all the copies are duplicated.
9 The system must not cost too much.

## Designing the system

Once you've produced your specification you can work out how data will move through the system.

Always start by thinking about what you want to come out of the system (you should do this whenever you're designing anything). From there you can work out what you need to put in and link the two together by describing the **processing stages** involved in producing the outputs.

Remember, you are designing the *whole* system so you will need to think about human processing as well as computer processing and the flow of data.

As you begin to work out the kind of processing the computer has to do you will need to make decisions about the kind of package or packages you will use. You should base you decisions on what type of package can do the job best. *Do* consider all possible approaches – the first one you think of might not be the best. It is certainly *not* a good idea to decide on the package first and then try to make the system design fit what this package can do.

For some systems you might need to use more than one software package – or you might choose an **integrated package** to allow you to move data easily between your word processor, your spreadsheet and your database. Don't be tempted to add extra parts to the system just to use more sections of the integrated package – stick to the system specification. For our newsletter system we will use a word processor to prepare text files, a scanner and scanning software to prepare picture files and DTP software to put the pages together.

You need to be very clear about how data will move through your system. You could describe this in writing or show it as a diagram like the one in Figure 14.1. This kind of diagram is called a **system flowchart**.

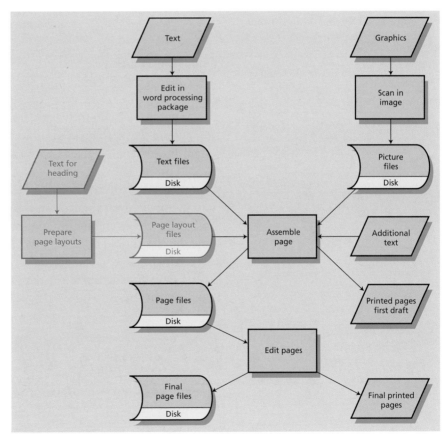

**Figure 14.1** *Here is an example of a system flowchart, showing how data flows through the system. This figure shows the system used for producing the school newsletter. The sections shown in red will only happen when the system is set up, but the sections in black will happen every time the newsletter is produced*

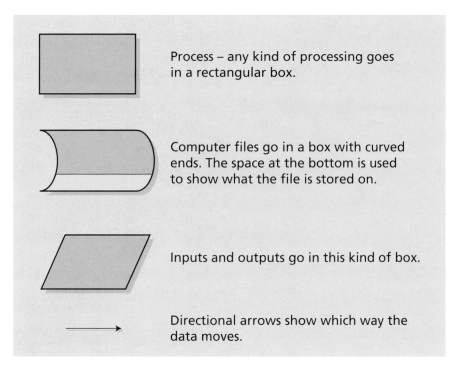

System flowcharts use certain shapes to represent input and output, processing and files stored on disk or tape – you can see some of these in Figure 14.2.

You will have to identify each main task you need to complete to make your system work. (The main tasks are the ones drawn in rectangles in the system flow chart.) Make a list of the main tasks then, once you've decided on the software and worked out how everything links together, you can get on with the detailed design work for each of the main tasks.

Remember, always start with the outputs needed and work out the inputs and processing requirements. When your design is complete someone else should be able to use it as a basis for setting up the system and getting it to work.

(We have already looked at design in detail in Chapters 3, 6, 9 and 12. Look back at these if you need to refresh your memory.)

## Designing the tests

Try to work out what tests you will need to test the whole system during the design stage. To test our newsletter system we will have to:

- prepare text files
- scan some pictures
- assemble one page of each type using the prepared outlines
- print each page
- rearrange the pages
- save the pages to disk
- print the newsletter in its final version.

**Figure 14.2** *Some of the symbols you will find on a system flowchart*

We will need to try text files of different sizes, and pictures of different sizes and types.

# Implementing the design

**Implementing** is setting up the system and making it work as it should. This is done using the software packages you have chosen – you will find this easiest if you tackle it one main task at a time. Always start with the essential tasks needed for the system (pretty introduction screens are not essential!) and as you complete each main task, test it to check that it works and that it matches the original specification.

The newsletter system is fairly simple but you will need to set up a **document template** for the word processor, so that you don't end up with different news items in different fonts and with different margins. You will also need to set up the scanner and scanning software for the kind of pictures you will be given – you might find that the scanner settings have to be different for different kinds of picture. Make a note of the settings that work best so you can put instructions in the **user guide** when you write it. You might be able to set up the software so that it always saves the picture files in the format you need.

The biggest task is creating the page layout files.

- You will have to put in the fixed heading on the layout for the first page.
- You will also have to set up the columns and fonts to be used on this page.
- You must then save this page.
- You must also create the layout file for the other pages in the same way.

# Testing the system

Testing must use three kinds of data (remember this from the chapter on databases?):

*Typical data* – to make sure it is handled as it ought to be. For the newsletter this will consist of short text files and small picture files.
*Data on boundaries* – to make sure the boundaries of the system are set correctly. For the newsletter this will consist of files too big to fit in a column and files too big to fit on a page.
*Data which is wrong* – to make sure **error trapping** works properly. For the newsletter this will consist of picture files in the wrong file format and text files which include unwanted fonts and the wrong margins.

| TEST NO | SELECTION TESTED | NATURE OF TEST | RESULT OF TEST (+ REFERENCE) |
|---|---|---|---|
| 1 | Data collection | Use all sheets to collect data | *Put results and comments here as testing done* |
| 2 | Entry of record | Valid data for all fields | *Include references to print outs* |
|  |  | Invalid data |  |
| 3 | Editing of record | Changes to each field existing |  |
| 4 | Deletion of record | Record no. to delete non-existent record number |  |
| 5 | Report production | Selection of report by name |  |
|  | TEST ALL REPORTS THIS WAY |  |  |
| 6 | Backup procedures | Do a backup |  |
|  | Recovery procedures | Restore a backup |  |
| 7 | User documentation | Get the user to work through the User Guide |  |

Table 14.1

You will need to prepare a **testing plan** to make sure that all the parts of your system are tested fully – without a plan you could miss out important aspects of testing. Testing the newsletter system is straightforward but other systems are more difficult to test fully. Table 14.1 shows how to plan for testing a database system.

When you are testing a system you will have to put some data into it. You must choose this data carefully to be sure that it will let you carry out all the tests you need and give you useful results. Write out your test data and the reasons you have chosen it. Check that it will let you test every possible way of using the system correctly, and all the possible ways of using it wrongly.

## TESTING THE WHOLE SYSTEM

In addition to testing that the tasks carried out by the computer work as they should, you will need to test the *entire* system when it has been put together to make sure that it all works properly together – this includes testing the human stages as well as the computer stages. You must prove that the system you have produced matches the system specification.

Testing must take into account all of the original specifications for the system. For example, if your system is supposed to be easy for young children to use, then your testing plan must include a session where young children try it out. You will need to test the newsletter system by asking the team producing the newsletter to try it out.

Good testing takes time, so if you are developing a system you should allow plenty of time for the testing stage – don't expect to do all the testing in a few minutes.

Record the results of your tests carefully, and get printouts to show what happens in the tests. The best way of doing this is to draw up a table to describe each test, what it is testing, the results you expect, and the results you get.

# *Documenting the system*

It is important to provide written information about your system (once it's working) so that other people can use it properly. This kind of written information is known as documentation. Two main types of documentation are usually provided with an IT system.

**Maintenance documentation** provides technical information about how the system was set up and how the parts are connected. It should include the test plans and results of the tests. It is designed to allow another competent person to look after the system and keep it up to date.

**User documentation** provides the person who will use your system with a set of instructions to tell them how to make the system work as it should.

When you write user documentation you will need to provide:

- Instructions for setting up the system
- Instructions, in a logical order, for normal use of the system
- Instructions for dealing with errors
- Instructions for making **copies** (backup copies) of all the data files and programs
- Instructions for recovering from a system failure – for example, if there is a power cut and some of the data files are lost.

Remember, you should test you user guide together with the system. The system won't be of any use if the users can't understand your instructions.

When you write the maintenance documentation for the newsletter system you should include:

- The system flowchart to show how data moves through the system
- Full details of how the word processing template document was set up, including margins, font selected and the text style
- Instructions on how to set up the scanning software (including scanner settings and file formats to be used to save picture files)
- The design sheets for the page layout with details of the heading text, its font, size and style
- Details of the fonts, sizes and styles you set up for the rest of the text on the page
- A list of file formats the package can accept and what it has been set up to expect.

All of this information would be very useful if you, or someone else, needed to make a few changes in the future.

In the user documentation for the newsletter system you would need to provide very clear instructions for carrying out every task.

- You would have to start by telling the user how to load the word-processing package and the text file template, then explain how to enter and save text.
- For the scanner and scanning software, after telling the user how to load the software, you would have to explain how to set the scanner for different kinds of picture and how to work the scanner and its software to scan the picture. Scanned pictures usually need some editing, so you should explain how to do this. You will have to provide clear instructions about saving the picture file in the right format.
- For the DTP package, you would need to explain how to load the package and then the page layout files for each kind of page. You would need to provide step-by-step instructions on how to put prepared text files into the page, how to put pictures into the page and also how to rearrange the page and change the size of pictures if necessary. You should include instructions for saving the finished page and also for printing the page.
- You also need to tell the user how to make backup copies of the files, and explain how to use the backup disks if the original files are ever lost.
- Your user documentation should also include a list of the problems the user's most likely to come across, what causes them and how to fix them.

# Summary

- Good systems design begins with analysing the users' requirements.
- When you know exactly what the user wants, produce a specification for the system. The specification will be the basis for checking that the system does everything it should.
- Work out ways of producing the system. Always look at alternatives and think about the advantages and disadvantages of the alternatives.
- Produce a plan to show how data will flow through your system.
- Design all the parts of the system.
- Implement the system using the packages you have selected.
- Test your system, making sure that all the parts work as they ought to. To do this you will need to construct a testing plan and select the right kind of test data.
- When you know your system is working properly, write your documentation. This usually includes maintenance documentation and a user guide.

# Questions

1 Write a description of each stage involved in producing an information system for someone else to use.

2 a Why is it important to produce a list of the requirements of a system?
  b What would you include in this list if you were developing a new system?
  c What uses would you make of this list?

3 a Why must testing of a system be planned carefully?
  b What are the general rules for selecting test data?
  c How would you present the results of testing a system?

4 A school is going to install a new computer controlled security system. Describe the main steps to be followed before the system is fully operational. (MEG)

5 A computer system is to be set up in a school laboratory.

  a Identify **two** safety issues which must be considered.
  b Describe **two** sensors which could be attached to the computer to collect data from experiments.

In the same school a database is used to store pupil data.

**Display A**

| SURNAME | FORENAME | GENDER | DATE OF BIRTH | YEAR GROUP | REGISTRATION GROUP | ADMISSION NUMBER |
|---|---|---|---|---|---|---|
| Robinson | John | Male | 12/03/80 | 11 | P | 23154 |
| Johnson | Paul | Male | 17/12/83 | 7 | F | 25013 |
| Maples | Jennifer | Female | 22/05/82 | 9 | P | 24438 |
| Wilson | Susan | Female | 18/01/80 | 11 | C | 23300 |
| Green | Paul | Male | 01/01/83 | 8 | C | 24881 |

Only some of the records and fields are shown.
This database can also produce a report like the one below.

**Display B**

**Pupil Information**

| | | | |
|---|---|---|---|
| Surname | Wilson | Gender | Female |
| Forename | Susan | Date of Birth | 18/01/80 |
| Other names | Jane | | |

**Parent/Guardian**

| | | | |
|---|---|---|---|
| Surname | Wilson | Forename | Brian |
| Title | Mr | | |
| Home Address | 23 Mills Place | Home Telephone | (01541) 785411 |
| | Stockley | Daytime Telephone | (01541) 765418 |
| | Cumbria | | |
| Postcode | ST30 9YZ | | |

**Medical Information**

| | | | |
|---|---|---|---|
| Doctor's Name | Dr P. Homer | Tel. Number | (01541) 776623 |
| Medical Conditions | Asthma | | |

**a** Before pupils enter the school, a form is sent home so that parents can provide the information needed for the database.

Produce a design for this form using the information in displays A and B to help you.

**6** A company uses mail order to sell its goods. A new computerised system is to be introduced.

  **a** Describe **two** steps involved in implementing the system.

  **b** Give **two** items of user documentation which would be supplied with the system. (MEG)

**7** A school office decides to change from typewriters to a computerised system. Describe **three** of the problems which will arise due to this decision being carried out.

**8** A school is introducing a computerised system for attendance registers. Describe the main stages gone through before the system is operational. (MEG)

# IT in a Medical Centre

*A typical Doctor's surgery*

| MALE | Surname | Fornames | |
|------|---------|----------|---|
| MALE | Address | | |
| Surname | | Forenames | |
| Date of Birth | | National Health Service No. | |
| Address | | Doctor's name | Committee's cipher & stamp |
| Tel. No. | | | |
| Subsequent address | | | |
| Tel. No. | | | |
| Tel. No. | | | |
| Tel. No. | | | |
| Tel. No. | | | |
| Occupations | Year | Note changes and insert year of change | Occupations | Year | FORENAMES | SURNAME |
| Date of death | | | | | | |
| Cause of death | | | | | | |
| Doctor's signature | | | | | | |

**Figure 15.1** *A record card from the Medical Centre*

In this chapter we shall be looking in detail at how a Medical Centre based in a small market town in the north-east of England uses IT. It is a group practice with five Doctors and about 9,000 patients, although this has varied between 7,000 and 12,000 as the population of the town varies.

## ■ *Before IT*

Before we look at the way IT was introduced into the practice, it may help us to look at the Centre before they had IT. When a patient first registered with the surgery, their personal details (name, age, sex) were taken, together with a 'medical life history'. These details were either collected from the patient themselves or from their previous Doctor. All of these details were written by hand and onto record cards, which were then filed away.

After a patient was seen by a Doctor, either in the Medical Centre or at home, details of the consultation were entered onto that patients' record card and a prescription for medicine written out and given to the patient if it was needed.

Prescriptions could be written for up to a month's supply of medicine, but some patients needed to be on medication for more than one month, and were given a repeat prescription. This involved the patient calling in to the surgery, either in person or by phone, or writing a letter each month. Then the Medical Centre clerks/receptionists had to find their notes and give them to the Doctor, who would then search through the information in the notes and decide to either write out the required prescription or ask to see the patient to review their progress.

The Doctors at the Centre also carried out immunisations against particular diseases, followed up chronic illnesses and gave advice as part of their normal procedure.

Sometimes tests would have to be carried out at the Centre and sent off to a hospital for analysis, then the results were sent back by post to the Medical Centre and written on the patients' record card.

If a patient went into hospital for any reason, notes relating to this would also have to be recorded by hand on the record cards.

# ■ *Introducing IT into the practice*

It is worth mentioning here how the Doctors are paid by the National Health Service. The payment they receive is made up of two parts:

First, a 'capitation payment' which is an amount of money for every patient on their practice's register. Secondly, 'item of service payments'. These are payments for particular things the doctors do. For instance, they are paid a certain amount of money for each night visit they carry out and for each immunisation they give.

These 'item of service payments' usually make up about 40% of a Doctor's income so obviously it is important to count the numbers of each item carried out accurately. Keeping a check on these items is very time consulting and sometimes inaccurate if carried out by hand.

A few years ago the Doctors decided to introduce IT into the practice, in order to make all areas of the medical practice run more efficiently, and therefore provide a better service to their patients.

For a number of years previously, several pilot studies using Information Technology in medical practices had been carried out where Doctors tried out the systems and suggested improvements so, hopefully, the systems introduced now would be more useful and reliable. Government, through the Department of Health, were trying to get medical practices to invest in Information Technology equipment, so there was lots of encouragement to try the new systems out.

**Figure 15.2** *The layout of the system chosen*

The main reason for change, however, was simple: to make the medical practice more efficient and provide a better service to their patients. You can see the system the Doctors chose in Figure 15.2.

It has nine terminals attached to the central processor. The software is easy to use and has been written specifically for medical practices. The menu in Figure 15.3 shows the major functions of the software.

Some of these functions are used every day, others are used less often (or not at all if they are not relevant to the practice). There is a database with a record for every patient registered at the Centre.

The screen in Figure 15.4 gives the major details of a particular patient.

Using this system the Doctor is also able to access two special database files. One is a conditions dictionary which gives information about a huge range of different diseases to help make a diagnosis. You can see a screen from this in Figure 15.5.

**Figure 15.3** *A screen showing major functions of the software*

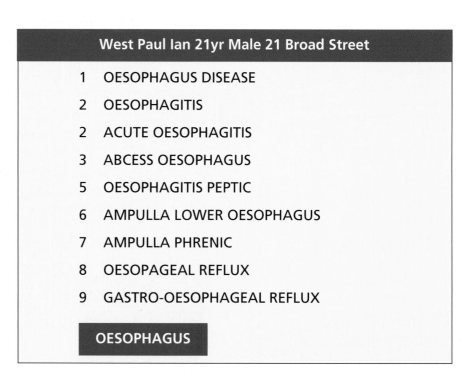

---

| West Paul Ian 21yr Male 21 Broad Street | | | |
|---|---|---|---|
| Prevention history verified | | ReG exam: Offered | 30/06/98 Due date |
| Major problems: | 13/07/95 | PAIN HIP | |
| | 16/07/95 | SLIPPED HIP EPIPHYSIS | ADMITTED |
| | 16/08/95 | SCREW FIXATION BONE | |

Repeat medication:

1. Allergy           No record
2. Intolerance:      No record
3. Contraception:    No record
4. Blood pressure:   No record
5. Smoking:          05/03/95 NON-SMOKER
6. Alcohol:          05/03/95 1 UNITS/WEEK
7. Recall:           No record
8. *Immun/Vacc:      1 DUE 1ST TPOL
9. *Weight/Height:   77.2Kg 05/03/94 180.3cm BMI: 23.7
10.Test results:     No record
11.InvestigAtions:   No record
12.Occupation:       No record

SELECT
A(dd)   B(ack)   G(raph)   N(ext)   P(rint HCC)   R(ecords)   S(creening)   <CR>   Exit

**Figure 15.4** *A screen showing a patient's major details*

The other is a drugs dictionary, which is updated every two months and, as you can see from the screen in Figure 15.6, contains information on each drug – the form it comes in (tablet, injection, liquid), the dosages (or strengths) available, the drug names (both general chemical names and brand names) and any other extra notes the Doctor may find useful.

---

### West Paul Ian 21yr Male 21 Broad Street

1   OESOPHAGUS DISEASE

2   OESOPHAGITIS

2   ACUTE OESOPHAGITIS

3   ABCESS OESOPHAGUS

5   OESOPHAGITIS PEPTIC

6   AMPULLA LOWER OESOPHAGUS

7   AMPULLA PHRENIC

8   OESOPAGEAL REFLUX

9   GASTRO-OESOPHAGEAL REFLUX

**OESOPHAGUS**

**Figure 15.5** *A screen from the conditions dictionary*

| | | | | |
|---|---|---|---|---|
| 1 | POW | 10.00% | | BUCLOSAMIDE/SALICYLIC ACID DIS DRUG |
| 2 | SOL | 10.00% | | BUCLOSAMIDE/SALICYLIC ACID DIS DRUG |
| 3 | CRE | 0.2% | | BUCLOSAMIDE |
| 4 | INH | 100meg | | BUCLOSAMIDE |
| 5 | INH | 200meg | | BUCLOSAMIDE |
| 6 | OIN | 0.2% | | BUCLOSAMIDE |
| 7 | SPR | 100meg | | BUCLOSAMIDE |
| 8 | INH | 50meg | | BUCLOSAMIDE |
| 9 | INH | 100meg | | BUCLOSAMIDE TURBOHALER |
| Date | Drug dictionary Name **BUCLOSAMIDE** | Form | Strength | |

**Figure 15.6** *A screen from the drugs dictionary*

# ■ *Getting used to the system*

When the computer system was installed in the Medical Centre, all the staff were trained for three days, including the two new clerks/receptionists who were employed to help run the system, by the company they bought it from. There then followed a six-month trial period before the system could be used properly. This let the Doctors and other staff get used to the ways of operating, as well as making sure the system worked properly.

The main task that had to be carried out was to transfer all the details from the record cards to the computer database files.

In order to get the system up and running in the shortest possible time, not all the details for each patient were transferred to the computer system at the same time. The information had to be summarised, then details were added in four distinct stages:

1 The first information to be transferred for each patient was the patient's name, date of birth, sex and address.
2 Once all of these details had been entered for each patient, data about any prescriptions the patient was receiving were added. This allowed the Centre to use the new prescription system, which we will look at later.
3 After this, details about any 'major life events' in terms of health were entered for all patients.
4 Finally, the data collected by the Doctors during their consultations with patients was put onto the database.

## ■ *How is the system used?*

The new computer system at the Medical Centre is used in many ways. The main use is to keep up-to-date records of every patient, which the Doctor can look up quickly and easily.

When the Doctors arrive in their consulting rooms at the Medical Centre, they are given a list of their appointments for the day which has been generated by the computer. In order to access information on the computer the Doctor has to type in a **password**, which only he or she knows, at the start of the session.

When a patient comes into the consulting room, the Doctor calls up the display for this patient by entering the patient's name (the full name does not have to be entered – if only the first few letters are typed then a list of patients in alphabetical order, starting from the letters typed is displayed and the Doctor can choose the correct one).

The information on the screen can be seen by the Doctor and is also visible to the patient. Sometimes the Doctor feels that the patient shouldn't see some details, and she uses a 'backscreen' facility on the display to hide these details and they do not appear on the screen.

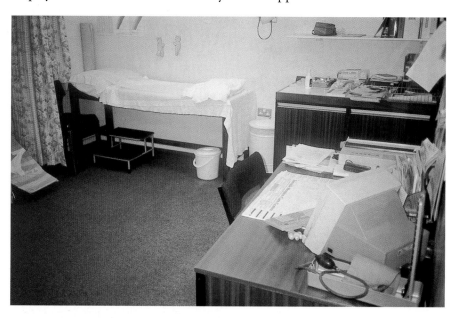

*A consulting room*

While talking with the patient, the Doctor can look up information in both the classification of drugs database and the conditions dictionary database if she needs to, although for more detailed information on a drug she would probably refer to the text book.

The Doctor can record details about the patient (perhaps their blood pressure) and, using data from several visits, can produce a graph on the computer to see if any trends are developing.

The Medical Centre still uses the old style record cards because the computer system doesn't allow the Doctors to enter detailed records and comments – it's also more time-consuming for the Doctor to type than it is to write. But some practices have moved across to completely computer-based records.

At the end of the consultation the Doctor enters brief details about it through the keyboard of the terminal – the date, the diagnosis and any medication prescribed. This data is stored automatically, updating that patient's computer record.

If the patient needs a prescription it can be printed out in the consulting room. This prescription can contain details which, under the old manual system, were never included, for example:

● details of the medication for the patient to tear off and keep,
● a date to return to the doctor for a review of the treatment,
● a message about a general health issue, such as the dangers of being overweight.

**Figure 15.7** *A sample prescription with tear-off information for the patient*

# How else is the system used?

The system is used by the practice in many other ways too. Here are a few.

## REPEAT PRESCRIPTIONS

When we looked at the situation before IT, there were times when a patient needed a repeat prescription. Each patient is now given a unique prescription number, which allows the clerk/receptionist to identify the patient and their prescription requirements. Each day the repeat prescription requests are processed, the prescriptions are printed and are given to the Doctor to sign. As she signs the prescriptions, the Doctor can use her terminal to check any patient details she needs. The prescription now contains the 'review' date for the treatment and if this date has been passed, the clerk/receptionist or the Doctor can ask the patient to make an appointment for a consultation.

## COMMUNICATION

The introduction of IT has also made it much easier to communicate with the thousands of registered patients. For example, patients may need to be screened (checked for a particular disease) every two years. With the old system it was extremely time-consuming to check through all the patient noted regularly to check when any of them might be due for a screening. But now it is possible to search the database files very quickly for every patient whose screening is due (say) in the next month and print out letters to every one of them to make an appointment. This can be applied to many other situations – for example, children need to have vaccinations at particular ages and the database files can be interrogated to find out which ones are needed and to produce letters to the parents of children whose immunisations are due.

Dr. M Evans
Dr. L. P. Naylor
Dr. A. Clark
Dr. D. W Gresham
Dr. J. F. Deakin
Dr. A. P. Connel
&DATE&

Health Centre
Fountain Road
Stockley
Cleveland
TS1 4NB
Tel: Ambleside 443

To the Parent/Guardian of:

&TITL&&INIT&&SURN&
&ADD1&
&ADD2&
&ADD3&

Dear Mr & Mrs  &SURN&

According to our records,  &FORN& is now due for Polio and Tetanus boosters.  An appointment has been made with Sister for your child to have this injection on  &APPT&

If this date is not convenient, please contact reception to arrange an alternative appointment.

Yours sincerely,

Dr. M. Evans

**Figure 15.8** *A sample immunisation reminder*

Another benefit of using a computer-based system is that a Doctor can print out an outline medical history of a patient and take it on visits to the patient's home.

## 'DRUG ALERTS'

Sometimes it is discovered that a particular drug has side effects, and the doctors need to find out which patients use, or have used, the drug. Before IT was introduced this would have taken a very long time and some patients might have been missed. But now the Centre can produce accurate lists of all the patients that have used this drug very quickly by searching for the drug in all the patients' records in the database file. The Doctors can also use the database to produce complex reports, perhaps linking the use of a particular drug to a particular side effect.

## MEDICAL RESEARCH

One of the major benefits of having all this data stored electronically is that details of diseases as well as the characteristics of the people suffering from them, the drugs and methods used to combat these conditions and details of how successfully they are, can be used to create a central database file which can be used for research purposes. For this to happen it is essential that the data sent is anonymous (the patient cannot be identified from the data) and has been verified (checked to make sure it is correct). About 800 medical practices provide this data, and the central database file now contains medical details of over two million anonymous patients. All these practices use the same file format for the data and actually send it on floppy disk.

# ■ *Keeping the data secure*

When you have so much personal data stored about people it is very important to make sure the data is not available to anyone who might use it to harm other people, or for their own advantage. There are strict laws and rules to prevent this including the Data Protection Act, which we shall look at in more detail in Chapter 18. In our example, the medical practice is registered as a data user with the Data Protection Registrar so it follows the regulations of the Data Protection Act.

They also have safeguards against unauthorised access to the database files in their system. All the Doctors and staff have their own password which they have to enter before they can use the system, and they also use **password hierarchies** to restrict access to data. All the terminals used by staff outside the consulting rooms are kept out of sight of 'passers by'. The system is completely contained in the building and is not connected to the telephone lines so no-one can get into the system from a computer outside.

It is also important to make sure that the data held on each patient is protected against accidental loss or damage so the Centre must make sure that it keeps copies of the data, which can be used to restore the database if it ever gets corrupted. Backup copies of the database files are taken each day for this purpose.

# ■ *Future developments*

Other medical practices now use systems that have been developed from the one we have looked at here. These systems are used to store, process and retrieve all patient details, including notes and comments, and there is an automatic check built in that tells the Doctor if a drug about to be prescribed to a patient clashes with another drug they're already taking.

In the near future, improvements in the way computers in different places can communicate will allow medical practice systems to have direct links to hospitals. This will mean, for example, that a patient's test results can be sent electronically from the hospital to the practice and will automatically update a patient's records. Note that this will have implications in terms of security. The test result data transmitted from the hospital to the practice in this example will have the patient's name included and when you have electronic links like this the system is opened up to the threat of hacking (more about hacking in Chapter 18).

In the future there will probably be direct links from medical practices to the Family Health Services Authority. Doctors will be able to send details of the number of patients registered with their practice, together with the 'item of service' totals for the FHSA to calculate the payments made.

# An Urban Traffic Control System

In this chapter we are going to look at the urban traffic control system that is in operation in the towns of Middlesbrough and Stockton-on-Tees in the county of Cleveland.

## ■ *What is an urban traffic control system?*

An urban traffic control system operates the traffic lights at road junctions and pedestrian crossings and controls the flow of traffic along these roads. The system we will be looking at in this chapter has three levels for operating the traffic lights and pedestrian crossings, which work at different times of the day.

### 'VEHICLE ACTIVATED' MODE

Traffic lights at a junction work as a set. During the evening they operate in 'vehicle activated' mode. Sensors built into the road near the junction detect when a vehicle is approaching the lights. If the lights are already on green for that vehicle then the lights won't change, but if they are on red

SENSORS

Vehicle activated mode sensors in the road detect vehicles approaching lights at junction

**Figure 16.1** *An urban traffic control system in vehicle activated mode*

Fig.(a) Traffic lights on green for road X and red for road Y

Fig.(b) vehicle pulls up at red lights on road Y, road X is still on green

Fig.(c) Lights on road X change to red, those on road Y change to green and the vehicle pulls away

**Figure 16.2** *A vehicle-activated traffic light system*

they will change to green. (The lights for the other roads entering the junction have to be changed first.)

## 'FIXED TIME' MODE

If the traffic flow gets heavier, the vehicle activated mode causes problems because the lights are changed too often. The system then switches to 'fixed time' mode. At each junction, a microprocessor contains a number of different plans to control the timing of the sequence of lights. The

**Figure 16.3** *Fixed time cycle*

particular plan used depends upon the time of day. The fixed time plans determine how long each part of the cycle of lights for each traffic light at the junction will last.

The amount of time the lights stay at point 1 and point 5 (Figure 16.3) depends on the plan, and the plan is based on a prediction of the average traffic flow through the junction at that particular time of day. The four plans used in Cleveland are:

- Peak a.m.
- Off-peak a.m.
- Peak p.m.
- Off-peak p.m.

The timings used in these plans were worked out using traffic surveys, then the times were programmed into the microprocessors at the junctions. These microprocessors, using the clock built into them, then select the correct plan for the time of day.

## PROGRAM CONTROLLED

The third method is computer controlled operation. Since 1985 the traffic lights and pelican crossings in the central areas of both Middlesbrough and Stockton-on-Tees have been controlled between 7 a.m. and 7 p.m. by a central computer sited in one of the County Council's offices in Middlesbrough.

Before we look at how the system operates, we need to see how the area controlled by the system is divided up.

Figure 16.4 *How the area is divided up*

# ■ *How the area is divided up*

The whole area covered by the system is split up into regions (as you can see in Figure 16.4). Each region contains a number of junctions. These junctions are called nodes and each one is given a code (for example N27). The nodes are the numbered boxes on the figure. The road between any two nodes in a particular direction is called a link and each link is given a code (like N27C – this shows that it is a link to node 27). At each node there is either a set of traffic lights (which are given a code starting with T – like T004) or a pelican crossing, which is given a code starting with P. There are 42 junctions and 22 pelican crossings under the central computer's control.

On each road leading to a junction (or node) that is controlled using this system, and at some distance from that junction, a detector is buried in the road. Every time a vehicle passes over this detector it sends a signal along a dedicated telephone line to the central computer. The computer knows the state (or colour) of the lights at that time and the average speed

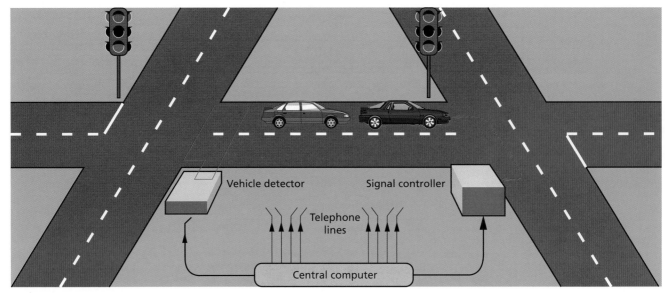

**Figure 16.5** *How the system works*

of a vehicle between the detector and the junction, and so can calculate the rate of flow of traffic for each road (or link) in and out of that junction.

# How the system works

At any time the state of the flow of traffic (called the 'link congestion') can be displayed on a screen in the control room in the County Council Office.

Figure 16.6 shows the link congestion for five regions which cover the centre of Middlesbrough. Each node or junction is given a number and has several arrows leading to and from it. The colour of the arrows indicates several things:

- Whether the traffic flow is normal (green arrow)
- Whether it's busy (yellow)
- If there is a queue (black)
- If there is congestion (red)
- If there is a fault (orange).

If a queue extends from one junction to another, the exit from one of these junctions will be blocked and this shows up on screen as a blue block. The information displayed on the screen is constantly updated.

In Figure 16.6 the flow of traffic through most junctions is normal. One link to node 2 is showing up as busy as are two links to nodes 20 and 22. You can see that the 'busy' flow is in the direction of Region A, which is the most central district of the town.

It is worth looking at node 27 in more detail. Of the four links leading into this junction, two are showing that the flow is normal, a queue is

**Figure 16.6** *Link congestion for the five regions covering the centre of Middlesbrough.*

forming in another and there is traffic congestion at the fourth. Only two links lead away from the node – the flow is normal in one and is busy in the other. As node 25 is close to node 27 the busy flow has caused this exit to be blocked at node 27.

The traffic controller can display a particular region in more detail (Figure 16.7). This figure displays the situation in Region A 13 minutes later. Each link now shows a code to identify it (for example, N27E), and the colour this code is displayed in indicates the state of the flow (link congestion). The arrows pointing at each node show the condition of the traffic lights, red or green. Now two of the links into node 27 (N27C and N27B) are congested and two (N27G and N27E) are normal.

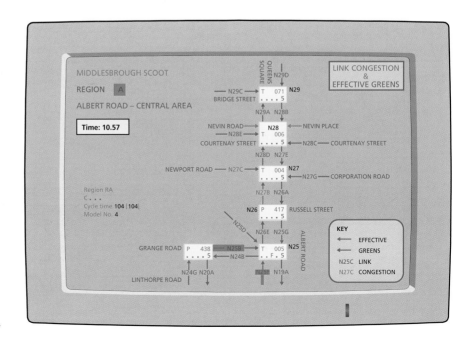

**Figure 16.7** *The situation in Region A.*

**Figure 16.8** *Node 27 with all the lights on red.*

The monitor in the control room can display a particular node instead of a region. Figure 16.8 shows node 27 at a point when all the traffic lights are on red and the crossings at this junction are allowing pedestrians to cross. Figure 16.9 shows the same node at a different point in the cycle – the traffic lights along Albert Road are on green and those on Corporation Road are on red.

Although these displays allow the traffic controller to see exactly what is happening in great detail, the computer program (not the controller) actually deals with the problems of congestion. The program takes into account all the data being fed into it, and tries to relieve the queues and congestion by altering, a little at a time, the timings of the lights.

**Figure 16.9** *Node 27 at another point in the cycle.*

The computer uses a technique called SCOOT (this stands for *Split Cycle Offset Optimisation Technique*), and the program in the central computer can alter the time any light is on a particular colour (the *split*), the time it takes for a set of lights to go through a complete cycle (the *cycle*) and the timings between different nodes (the *offset*). The controller can change the timings manually, but doesn't do it very often, usually only when accidents occur or when there are roadworks in the area.

# ■ *What happens if the system fails?*

If the computer system fails, the traffic lights automatically go back to operating in 'fixed time' mode. If faults occur, the condition shows up on the various screen displays and a buzzer sounds in the control room. These faults are logged by the computer and can be printed out at any time. At 3 a.m. the computer program checks all parts of the system (detectors, lights, etc.) for faults and the results of these tests are logged and printed out so that the engineers can trace any faults and repair them.

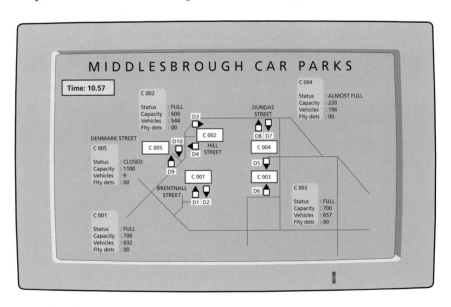

**Figure 16.10** *Car park monitoring.*

# ■ *Car parking*

This computer system also controls the information signs about car parks in the town centre. Detectors in the road at the entrances and exits of the car parks send signals back to the central computer which can then count the number of vehicles in each car park. The computer also stores the total number of vehicles each car park can accommodate and sends signals to the electronic signs to display each car park's status – whether it has spaces, how full it is or whether it is closed.

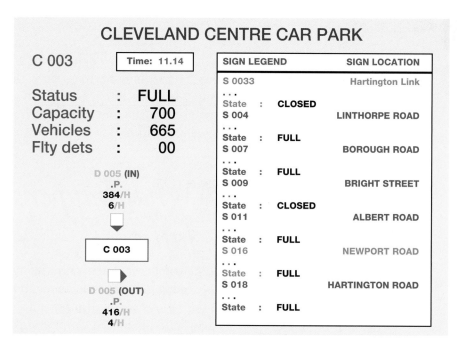

Figure 16.11 *Another display used to monitor car parks*

Figure 16.12 *The screen showing the display on the car park sign and the actual sign*

Diagrams displayed on the monitor can show the details of all the car parks in an area or details of each car park separately. These displays give the status, the capacity of the car park, the number of vehicles currently parked and the number of faulty detectors. The screen for one particular car park also shows the message that's being displayed on electronic information signs in the area, regarding its state. Exactly what is being displayed on each of these signs can also be shown on the screen.

## Questions

1 The traffic light system of a large town is to be computerised. The lights at many junctions are to be controlled by a single central computer.

   a Give two types of input required for the system
   b Give two benefits of introducing the system.

# IT in a Supermarket

Today, IT is vital to the retail business in general, and to supermarkets in particular. In a large modern supermarket computers are used in many different ways, from controlling the stock to controlling the temperatures in fridges and freezers. In this chapter we will take a detailed look at these uses in a large supermarket which is one branch of a national chain.

Our supermarket uses several computers, which are kept in a room called the system office. One of these computers is used to control the stock and is connected to each checkout. We shall call this the 'branch computer'.

Each checkout has an **electronic point of sale (EPOS)** till, and each EPOS till has the following:

- a keyboard
- a digital display
- a scanner to read bar codes
- a set of scales
- a printer
- a credit/debit card reader
- a till drawer.

All of these parts are attached to the base unit of every till. The base unit is connected by cables to the branch computer in the system office.

## ■ *Bar codes*

Every product on sale must have an identifying code number different from that of every other product. Different sizes of the same product need different code numbers as well. These numbers are printed onto the labels or packaging of the product as bar codes (you can see an example of a bar code in Figure 17.1).

A bar code contains four pieces of data:

- The code for the country the company producing the product comes from. The code for the UK is 50.
- The code for the company which produces the product – 00314 in the example in Figure 17.1.
- The code for the product – 40052 in our example.
- A check digit, to make sure that the bar code has been read correctly.

Nearly all grocery products now have a bar code.

**Figure 17.1** *A bar code*

**Q**

The bar code for the UK is 50. Find out the codes for

Germany
France
Any other country

Collect some bar codes and try to identify the country code and the company code for each one

Why doesn't the bar code on a tin of soup contain its price?

**Q**

Which two scanning devices would allow bar codes to be read most quickly?

Why?

# Scanners

The bar codes on products are read by the infrared beam on the scanners at the EPOS till. Scanners come in many different forms. Here are four of them:

- wand
- gun
- horizontal scanner
- flat bed scanner.

**Figure 17.2** *The types of scanning devices that are used to read bar codes*

This particular supermarket uses flat bed scanners. When an item is passed over the scanner, a sequence of events happens very quickly:

1 It reads the bar code and sends the number it represents to the branch computer.
2 The branch computer uses the number to look up the product record in a file. The record contains the price and a description of the product.
3 This data is sent back to the EPOS till at the checkout.
4 The till shows the item and price on the digital display, prints them on a receipt and adds the price to the total.
5 At the same time the branch computer records what has been sold.

When a bar code has been scanned properly, the scanner makes a beeping sound – if this sound isn't made, the item must be passed over

```
          SAVEMORE
     QUALITY AT LOWEST PRICES


                           £
  K/ORA WHOLE ORANGE       2.19
  S/PINK T/TISSUE X 9      2.49
  S T/TISSUE GRNX9         2.49
  AMB DEVON CUSTARD        0.49
  D.M FRUIT COCKTAIL       0.63
  MANDARINS + SYRUP        0.48
  S P/PEACH SLICES         0.37
  TOMATO JUICE             1.29
  HZ TOMATO KETCHUP        0.74
  S S+V CRNCHY STICK       0.42
  WALLFAN WAFERS           1.09
  C/CLASSIC MINT           0.54
  S MINI PIZZAS X 10       1.19
  S MILD CURE HAM          1.55
  S LAMB CUTLETS           1.02
  F/F HAGGIS               2.52
  1.57LB @ £0.59LB
  APPLES EMPIRE            0.93
  S SALMON                 1.65
  HZ TOMATO SOUP           0.32
  HZ TOMATO SOUP           0.32
  HZ TOMATO SOUP           0.32
  HZ TOMATO SOUP           0.32
  WALL VIENNETTA           1.09
  S SZ3 EGGS X 18          1.74
  MORN OAT+NUT CRNCH       0.55
  MORN OAT+NUT CRNCH       0.55
  S SIRLOIN STEAK          3.51
  LEMON LS                 0.18
  S MARGARINE              0.75

  ****     TOT            31.73

  CASH                    40.00
  CHANGE                   8.27

  31/05/98   12.28   0667   02 66

   THANKYOU FOR SHOPPING WITH
            SAVEMORE
```

**Figure 17.3** *An itemised till receipt.*

the scanner again until the bar code has been read correctly. The operator uses the keyboard to enter codes of products that won't scan, for example reduced price items.

The scales at the EPOS till are also linked to the branch computer. All loose fruit and vegetables are weighed at the checkout and the product's code number is typed at the keyboard to give the customer a description of the product on the receipt, together with its weight and price (you can see an itemised receipt, containing this sort of information in Figure 17.3).

The printer attached to the EPOS till can print cheques and debit/credit card vouchers as well as printing an itemised receipt. This makes mistakes much less likely, and saves time.

## Transferring funds electronically

Many people now choose to pay by credit or debit card rather than cash. The customer's card is passed through the card reader, which reads the data (usually the account number and date of expiry) on the magnetic strip on the back of the card. The data from the magnetic strip of a debit card is then used, together with details of the amount spent, to transfer this amount from the customer's bank account to the supermarket's bank account. This process is called **electronic funds transfer (EFT)** and works even if the supermarket's bank and the customer's bank are different.

## Stock control

In fact, two branch computers are linked to the EPOS terminals at the checkout. They both store the data about items sold and act as backup for each other. Imagine what would happen if only one computer was used and it broke down.

These branch computers are linked via telephone lines to a large main computer at the supermarket's head office in another part of the country. The computers at all the branches are linked to the main computer like this.

After the supermarket has closed at the end of the day, the branch computer sends the details of every sale to the main computer at head office. The main computer system uses this data to update the records of the stock of every item in each store. It uses a forecast of sales along with other factors (such as the weather or time of year) to automatically order the correct amount of stock needed by each store for the next day. The main computer also transmits these orders to computers in the distribution centres. These are large warehouses storing products ready for delivery. The distribution centres deliver the stock to the stores immediately.

At the same time as the branch computers send their sales data to the main computer, the main computer sends back any price changes, descriptions of new items and details of any special offers to each branch.

In addition to being used for stock control, the sales data is stored by the main computer at the head office to build up a 'profile' or description of the way its customers shop. For example, the proportion of customers who use powder compared with those who use liquid detergent can be worked out from the sales of washing detergents in any particular store. This sort of information can be used to work out how much shelf space each product should have.

# Pricing

The branch computer holds the price of each product and sends it to the EPOS terminal when the product's bar code is read. The package doesn't show the price, and doesn't have a price label – the only place where the price is displayed is on a label attached to the shelf near the product (like the one in Figure 17.4).

**Figure 17.4**  *The type of shelf label you are likely to see in a supermarket.*

It used to be that every single item had its own price label, which meant that when the price changed new labels had to be stuck on top of the old ones. This took quite a long time to do, as every item on the shelves affected by the price change had to be relabelled, and any mistakes meant that customers would be overcharged or undercharged. Now, when price changes are sent from the head office computer to the branch computer during the night, new shelf labels are printed and the night staff in the supermarket put these on the shelves ready for the next day.

| BUY | GET |
|---|---|
| Grunt's Finest Scotch Whiskey | Curly Black Label Lager |
| 1 litre    **£13.99** | 4 x 500ml    **£2.79** |

*Co SAVE*

**Figure 17.5** *A special offer label*

Special offers – like 'Buy two and get one free' or 'Buy one product and save 50% on another' – couldn't be offered easily before the introduction of IT. Now, as the bar codes are scanned, the branch computer looks for items on special offer and discounts the prices where necessary.

## Freezers and chiller cabinets

Computers are also used to control the freezers and chiller cabinets throughout the store. The large freezers in the warehouse have to be kept within a certain temperature range. This is done using temperature **sensors** inside each freezer to monitor the conditions. Data from these sensors is sent to the computer and it switches the cooling motors on and off.

*Freezer and chiller cabinets are a common sight in today's supermarkets.*

*The kind of display you are likely to see on a chiller cabinet.*

On the floor of the supermarket many freezers and chiller cabinets are used to store and display a wide variety of products such as fresh meat, dairy produce and frozen goods. Different products need to be stored at different temperatures – fresh meat, for example, may have to be kept at 4°C while ice cream has to be kept at −15°C. In the past, an employee had to check the temperature of each freezer and chiller cabinet every hour. Now they are all linked to a computer in the branch office. A temperature sensor in each freezer and chiller constantly sends back data to the computer, which sends signals back to switch the individual freezer and chiller motors on and off, maintaining the correct temperatures. A display on each cabinet shows the temperature to the customers.

Each chiller and freezer has to be defrosted every three or four hours, and the computer controls this process. Any breakdowns are detected immediately, which reduces the risk of food thawing and being wasted.

## Loyalty cards

The supermarket, like many of its competitors has recently introduced a loyalty card. It hopes that these cards will help keep customers faithful to this supermarket and increase their spending.

When a customer applies for and obtains a card, they are given a unique membership number. Every time they spend money in the supermarket, they are awarded a number of points. These points are recorded and add up each time they visit the supermarket. Points can be exchanged for cash, free products or discount on a variety of consumer goods and services.

For the supermarket, these cards have the bonus of producing a shoppers database. When a customer applies for a card, the customer fills in an application form which gives the supermarket the beginning of a profile for that customer. For example, they will know where the customer lives, whether the customer is male or female and their age range.

Each time the customer uses their loyalty card, the details of what they bought and when they bought it are recorded on their record in the customer database. This data helps the supermarket get a better understanding of their customers and is used in many ways. Shopping patterns can be analysed to allow the supermarket to look at their opening times and how many checkouts should be used at any particular time of day. Special offers can be sent to customers about products which the supermarket now knows that they buy on a regular basis.
The supermarket believes that collecting and using this data will build up a relationship between the customer and itself and allow them to provide a better and more profitable service.

## PORTABLE SHOPPING SYSTEMS

Supermarkets are getting busier. At the same time, people want to spend less time in the supermarkets. Traditionally, customers push their trolleys up and down aisles of products until they have obtained all the goods they wish to buy then head off to the checkouts. Even with EPOS tills, the queues can be lengthy and the wait quite long.

When customers obtain their bill, the total amount can often be higher than they thought as they had no way of knowing how much they were spending as they were putting items in their trolleys.

Our supermarket has recently introduced a new system to try and cut down the queues at checkouts and prevent customers from getting unexpectedly high bills.

This new system uses a hand held scanner, the portable shopper, which is about the shape and size of a telephone handset. This is how the customers use the system:

After entering the supermarket, the customers go to a rack containing a number of these hand held scanners. After inserting their loyalty card into a slot in the rack, they pick up the scanner on which a light is flashing. The scanner can be held in the hand or put into a special holder on the trolley.

*A Portable shopping system scanner*

*Scanning a bar code*

The scanner has three buttons, 'plus', 'minus' and 'equals' as well as a light and a small visual display.

When the customer selects a product, he or she presses the 'plus' button. This starts the laser which the customer scans over the bar code on the product to record the purchase in the memory of the scanner. If the scan was successful, the light on the scanner turns green and the price of the product is shown on the visual display. If the scan was unsuccessful, the lights stays red and the item needs to be rescanned.

As bar codes do not contain prices, these are downloaded from the supermarket's main computer to each hand held scanner whilst they are in their rack at the start of each day.

If the customer decides against buying a product but has already scanned it, it can be cancelled by using the 'minus' button to rescan the item's bar code. This deletes the purchase from the memory of the scanner.

The total cost of all the purchases recorded can be obtained at any time on the visual display by pressing the 'equals' button.

When the shopping is complete, the customers return their scanner to the rack which automatically produces a bar coded ticket. The customer then takes this ticket to an express checkout where a member of staff scans the ticket, any items which the customer's scanner was not able to scan and accepts any coupons. Customers pay as usual, receive the normal itemised receipt and are on their way.

Occasionally, the ticket produced at the rack asks the customer to get all their items rescanned at a normal EPOS till. This is to try to prevent shoplifting.

Customers do not have to use this personal shopping system. They can shop and get all their items scanned at the end by using the EPOS checkouts as usual.

# Advantages of IT in a supermarket

The advantages of using IT in supermarkets can be broken down into two sections:

- the benefits to the customers
- the benefits to the supermarket management.

Remember that changes and improvements come out over a period of time. While the introduction of IT will eventually save the supermarket chain money, a good deal of investment, both in terms of resources and training, is needed. This does not happen just at the start but throughout the development of the new system.

## ADVANTAGES TO THE CUSTOMER

Customers will find that IT makes their shopping easier in many ways.

- The checkout services are faster and more efficient.
- Till receipts are itemised, so they can check prices and see if any mistakes have been made.
- The products are more tailored to their needs.
- The goods are fresher because stock levels held by supermarkets can be lower.
- There are more special offers.
- The benefits to the supermarket are passed on through lower prices or better customer services.
- Various methods of payment are allowed, so they don't have to carry cash.
- Chilled and frozen foods are kept at the correct temperature, so health hazards are much lower.

## ADVANTAGES TO THE SUPERMARKET AND MANAGEMENT

IT also brings a number of advantages to the store management.

- Stock control is more efficient, so there is less chance of goods being out of stock.
- The checkout is more efficient and there is less chance of staff making errors.
- Sales forecasts and profiles can be made, which leads to more efficient use of shelf space.
- Little warehouse space is needed in each supermarket because of the efficient distribution system.

- The performance of the checkout staff can be monitored.
- Shelf pricing is more cost effective than labelling each product separately.
- The ability to use electronic funds transfer improves cash flow.
- Chilled and frozen goods can be managed effectively.

## Questions

**1** Not all shops use computerised systems like the one described in this chapter. Explain why such a system would be unlikely to be used in a small greengrocer's shop.

**2** Tick **two** benefits to shoppers of using point-of-sale machines at supermarket check-outs.

| | |
|---|---|
| Shopping bills can be calculated. | |
| Itemised receipts can be produced. | |
| Shopping can be packed by an assistant. | |
| Prices are printed on all the goods. | |
| The assistant does not have to key in the prices. | |
| Customers can pay for their goods using a cheque. | |

(MEG)

**3** Discuss the advantages and disadvantages of using Information Technology in shopping. (MEG)

**4** The diagram shows an itemised receipt from a supermarket which uses a Point of Sale (POS) system.

```
        SUPERSAVE
        10/03/96

Flour 1 kg        0.69
Rice              0.45
White Bread       0.42
Total             1.56
```

**a** How is data about the items bought entered into the system?
**b** Where is the price held to produce the receipt?
**c** Give **two** advantages **to the customer** of the use of this system.
**d** Give **two** advantages **to the manager** of the use of this system. (NEAB)

# C H A P T E R

# IT and Society

The introduction of IT on a large scale has had far-reaching effects on society. Some of these have been unpopular, but many have been beneficial. As the effects have caused concerns, laws have been introduced to control the use of data stored in computer-readable form and deal with theft of and damage to data.

## ■ *Controlling data use*

The law gives people the right to see any data about themselves which is stored on computer. If the data is wrong they have the right to make sure it is changed or removed from the database.

People and firms that store data about living people have to obey certain rules.

- They must make sure the data is collected in a fair way and that it's only used for the purpose for which it was collected. To make sure they don't suddenly invent new purposes they have to register that they are using the data, describing what they will be using it for and how they will get the data. Data collected for a particular purpose must be just what is needed for that purpose. It is not legal to collect lots of data about people when it is not relevant to the task that is going to be carried out.
- Once the data has been collected the data user must see that it is kept up to date and when they have finished with it the data must be destroyed.
- While the data is stored it must be protected from accidental loss or alteration by keeping backup copies in a safe place. Data must also be protected from deliberate damage or theft so companies using data must have good security systems (such as passwords) to be able to read and alter files. Doors to rooms containing storage media and computer systems must be kept locked. The more sensitive the data is, the more important it is that the protection is effective.
- Data can't be given away or sold unless the intention to do this has been stated. Companies who want to sell data can do so but must tell the person concerned that this is one of the things they want to do with the data when it is collected.

Even when companies work within these rules, some of their activities can annoy some people. A great deal of information is available freely and legally. Sources include:

- the electoral register
- telephone directories
- the Royal Mail database of postal addresses
- lists of property valuations for the council tax.

Some of this information is available on paper but quite a lot can be supplied as data in computer-readable form. Individually, these databases may not provide much information but if the data from several is combined then a great deal can be worked out about an individual. Various mail order operators and subscriptions departments of magazines and clubs will sell information on their databases (they get permission to pass on information by asking their customers to indicate if they do not want it passed on to firms selling similar products). **Credit reference agencies** also supply information about a person's ability to repay loans.

With all this data stored in database files, it's quite easy to build up a detailed personal profile on someone. This could include:

- name
- address
- age group (possibly date of birth)
- family details
- the value of the house they live in
- whether they own or rent their home
- information on income and credit rating
- information on buying habits.

Combining data like this isn't illegal as long as the resulting database is notified, but it's very unlikely that anyone would ever know that a particular firm had all this data on them. To check that the data stored is accurate and up to date a person needs to know who holds the data.

Data from these databases is often sold as lists to companies who want to use **direct mailing** or **telesales** to sell their products. The lists can be selected to include certain types of people – those in a certain age group, or a particular income band, or with a history of buying similar products, for example. Although these uses can be annoying they don't actually do any real harm. But the personal profiles could be used as the basis of discrimination, sometimes on the basis of faulty conclusions from out of date or incorrectly interpreted information.

**Q**

**What rights does the Data Protection Act give to members of the general public?**

**Data users have to make sure that while the data is stored, it must be protected from accidental loss or alteration. Give one method of achieving this.**

**How can data be protected against deliberate damage or theft?**

# ■ *Hacking*

**H**acking is the term used to describe the process of illegally **accessing** and sometimes altering data stored in a computer system. The person who does it is called a **hacker**. Even if they don't damage the data, if a person who has no right to see the data looks at it they are committing a criminal offence. Often, even if there is no intention of damaging the data in the system, data is lost because the hacker handles it wrongly – and sometimes the hacker intends to alter the data. Altering the data can lead to substantial losses to the owner of the data – which is often what the hacker intends to happen. It is very important that data is accurate – in some applications it is vital. Hackers have been known to alter the data in hospital systems and change patient records and prescriptions – luckily, so far, the changes have been detected before any harm was caused.

# Data software and theft

## DATA THEFT

Data and programs stored in computer-readable form can be copied quickly without leaving evidence that they have been copied. Data is often valuable and could be very sensitive, so it must be protected from attempts to make illegal copies.

The best way of doing this is to convert the data to a coded form using an **encryption** program. The program alters the data in a complex way so that, without knowing the exact method of encryption, it is impossible to restore the original data. So encrypted data is useless to a thief.

## SOFTWARE THEFT

Theft of software is a major problem. People who wouldn't normally dream of committing a crime often make extra copies of computer programs so they can use them on more machines, use them at home, or give them to friends. This means that the author of the program loses income from selling more copies of the program – and it is illegal.

Computer software must be sold in a usable form, so encryption can't be used to protect these programs. Business users also expect to be able to make backup copies of the programs they use (which is legal), so the kind of copy-protection methods often used for computer games can't be used.

Large-scale copying and sale of computer software has been known. These cases have involved both business software and games. Sale of these illegal copies (usually much cheaper than the original program) represents a huge loss to the computer industry.

Software users who steal programs like this are damaging the industry. It takes a long time and costs a lot of money to develop a commercial software package. If the company making such a package doesn't get the income they expect from a program because it is being copied and sold illegally they won't be able to pay for developing new packages.

# Summary

- Data stored in computer-readable form can be used in ways not possible with data stored on paper.

- A law has been introduced to control the use of data in computer-readable form.

- Laws have also been introduced to deal with data theft and damage.

- Data has to be collected fairly and lawfully.

- Data stored on computer must be accurate and up to date.

- A person can see the data stored about them and change it if it is wrong.

- Data must only be used for the purpose it was collected for.

- Data must be kept secure.

- Accessing and altering data without the right to do so is a crime.

- Data can be protected by encryption.

- Making extra copies of programs and selling them, using them on additional machines or giving them to friends is a crime.

## Questions

1 Describe how computers might be misused giving rise to legal and moral problems. (MEG)

2 a Describe **two** ways the Data Protection Act tries to protect individuals from the misuse of personal data held on computer.
   b Other than the misuse of personal data, describe **two** ways in which Information Technology has created problems for the individual. (MEG)

3 'It is easier to misuse data when it is held in electronic form.'

   Discuss this statement. (MEG)

4 A hacker may gain access to a school computer system. Describe **three** ways in which this could affect the school. (MEG)

5 Discuss the effects of IT on employment. (MEG)

6 The widespread use of IT has had a great impact on today's society. One benefit that the increased use of IT has brought, is the creation of some new jobs.

   **a** Give **three examples of jobs** that have been created by the introduction of IT.

   **b** Describe briefly **three other** possible benefits that this increased use in IT has brought.

   **c** Personal information, stored electronically, is potentially easier to misuse than that kept in paper files. Give **two** reasons why this is true. (NEAB)

**7** Mail order catalogue companies use computer systems to hold a large amount of personal information about their customers.
Give **three** items of data (other than name and address) which they may reasonably hold. (NEAB)

**8** Information Technology is now used in many ways by Banks and Building Societies. Describe ways in which the introduction of Information Technology has had an effect on:

   **a** staff of the Banks and Building Societies;
   **b** customers of the Banks and Building Societies.

**9** Many schools now store personal information about their pupils on computer systems.
Give **three** items of personal data (other than name and address) which they may reasonably hold. (NEAB)

**10** Robots are used in many manufacturing processes, particularly in the car industry.

   **a** State **three** advantages of using robots in the manufacturing of cars.
   **b** State **two** disadvantages of using robots in the manufacturing of cars. (NEAB)

**11** Many organisations, such as police, banks and schools now store personal information on computer files rather than on paper files.
Give **three** reasons why it might be easier to misuse information stored electronically rather than the same information stored on paper files. (NEAB)

**12** Discuss the issues raise by the use of IT in society. Your answer should cover a number of different areas, taking into account the environmental, ethical, moral and social effects. You should highlight possible disadvantages as well as advantages. (NEAB)

# Glossary of terms used in the text

**accessing**   Reading data from a computer file, or writing data to a computer file

**algorithm**   A plan showing the steps needed to solve a problem or carry out a task

**analogue (value)**   A quantity which varies continuously, without fixed gaps between values. An example is temperature

**aural (information)**   Information which is heard

**backup copy**   A copy of computer-readable data stored on a separate disk or tape, to be used if the original is lost or damaged

**backing store**   The disk, tape or other medium used to hold computer-readable data. Data stored here is not lost when the computer is switched off

**binary number**   A number consisting only of ones and zeros

**blocks (of text)**   A portion of a document which is marked and then handled as a single unit.

**boundaries (of a system)**   The limits of a system. A statement of what the system will do and what it will not do.

**buffer box**   An interface used to connect sensors to a computer

**calibrate (a sensor)**   To match readings from a sensor to an accepted scale in known units

**CD-ROM**   An optical disk used to store a large amount of computer-readable data. The data can be read but not changed.

**cell**   A single box or location in a spreadsheet

**cell address**   The column letter and row number which identify a particular box in a spreadsheet

**centre (text)**   To place text symmetrically between the left and right margins, for example in a word processed document

**changing margins**   To change the amount of space left at the edges of a document. If text is already present it will be rearranged

**charting package**   A package designed to produce graphs and charts from data entered by the user

**chip**   An electronic circuit, on a small slice of silicon, designed to do a particular job

**clip-art**   Ready-made pictures and diagrams, stored on disk, which can be used to illustrate documents

**column width**   The number of characters that can be fitted in the cells in a column of a spreadsheet

**computer aided design (CAD) package**   A software package for producing detailed technical plans and drawings, and for doing calculations

**computer aided manufacture (CAM) package**   Using a computer program to control the production of an object by a machine

**constraint (in a system)**   Limits imposed in system design – such as cost limits, availability of hardware and software

**context**   The situation in which data becomes information

**copy (a disk or file)**   To duplicate the computer-readable data onto another disk

**corruption (of a disk or file)**   Altering data so it is either unusable or unreadable

**credit reference agency**   A firm which keeps records about the financial status of people, to supply information to others

**cursor**   A small box, arrow, line or cross which shows the current position on the screen

**data** Information removed from its context and encoded for computer use

**data-logging** collecting and storing data at regular, fixed intervals over a period of time

**database** A collection of files which can be searched or processed in a variety of ways to produce different outputs

**data table** Alternative name for a file in a relational database

**database report** The printed output from a database

**deleting (text)** Removing unwanted text from a document

**desktop publishing (DTP)** Page layout software which allows text and graphics to be combined in a variety of ways

**digital** Consisting of distinct numbers

**direct mailing** Advertising by sending letters straight to people, without having been asked to supply information

**distorting (sounds)** Adding noise, or altering the length of a sound to change it in some way

**document** A letter, report or other piece of work produced using a word processing package

**document template** Standard settings for documents. These can be saved on disk and re-used

**documentation** Written information about a computer system. It is usually divided into **user documentation** and **maintenance documentation**

**documenting** Writing the user and maintenance instructions for a computer system

**double spacing** Leaving a blank line between lines of text in a document

**drawing package** A package used to produce line drawings. It handles each piece of the drawings as a separate object

**duplicate (part of a drawing)** Automatically producing multiple copies of an object or group of objects in a drawing

**EFT** Electronic funds transfer, used to transfer money between accounts immediately

**EPOS** Electronic point of sale system, used in shops to read bar codes and look up prices, often linked to stock control systems

**Email** Using computers to transfer messages between users. Messages are held in a central store until read.

**encryption** Altering data stored on disk or transmitted from one computer to another so that it makes no sense if it is stolen

**end-user** The person who will eventually use an information technology system

**error trapping** Detecting and handling data that's been input wrongly in a way which allows the computer program to continue to run

**evaluate (software)** Deciding how well a software package carries out a given task

**feedback** Continuous use of data from sensors to control the output of a computer system

**field** A single data item in a record

**field length** The number of characters that can be fitted into a field

**field type** The kind of data which can be stored, for example numbers, characters, true/false

**file** A collection of related records

**file format** The way data in a file is stored on disk

**fill (a shape)** To colour in the inside of a drawing on the screen with a selected shade

**format (of a spreadsheet cell)** The way the data in the cell is displayed

**formula** The method for carrying out calculations in a spreadsheet. The formula contains the addresses of cells used in doing the calculation

**frame** A rectangular shape used in DTP packages. Text or graphics can be placed in it and the frame contents are handled as a single object

**full justification** Spacing is adjusted so that the text is spread out to fill a whole line, so both left and right edges of the text make straight lines

**function (in a spreadsheet)** A predefined method of carrying out a calculation – for example working out an average

**grading (a fill)**   Altering the shade of the filling colour from light to dark. This can make objects look more curved or three-dimensional

**graphics**   Any kind of drawings or charts included in a document, or produced on their own

**group (of objects)**   Several objects, in a drawing, which are collected together and linked so that they can be handled as if they were just one thing

**hacker**   A person who makes illegal access to a computer system

**hacking**   The process of gaining illegal access to a computer system

**heading area**   The area of a database report containing data which is printed at the top of each page of the report

**hypertext link**   Text which provide links to other pages in an information store

**icon**   A small picture representing an action available to the user of a package. Icons are selected using a mouse

**implementing**   Setting up a computer-system and ensuring that it runs properly

**importing (data/files)**   Loading data, or whole files, produced using one software package, into another software package

**information**   Data placed in a context so that it has meaning

**information retrieval**   Getting data out of computer-readable files and putting it into context so that it can be understood by users

**inserting (text)**   Adding extra text into a word processed document

**integrated package**   A set of programs, usually including a word processor, a spreadsheet and a database, designed so that data can be moved easily between the different sections

**interface unit**   A piece of hardware which allows communication between a computer and devices such as sensors attached to it

**Internet**   A worldwide network of networks

**Intranet**   Pages of information similar to the World Wide Web which can only be accessed over a LAN

**justification**   The way text or other data is arranged in the space available

**landscape orientation**   Arranging the page layout so that the document is short and wide

**layer (of a drawing)**   One level in the drawing. The objects drawn at this level can be moved so that they are in front of or behind things drawn on different levels

**left justification**   Arranging the contents of a line of text, or other data, so that the left edge is straight. The right-hand edge is not straight

**line spacing**   The amount of space left between lines of text. Single spacing leaves less space than double spacing

**Local Area Network (LAN)**   A network in which the component parts are linked by cables

**LOGO**   A computer programming language with commands which can be used to control movement of a screen turtle or of an external device

**magnetic disk**   A thin, circular piece of metal or plastic, coated with a material which can be magnetised. Data is stored by magnetising tiny spots in different directions

**magnetic tape**   A long thin strip of plastic tape, coated with a material which can be magnetised. Data is stored as magnetised spots arranged across the tape

**mail merging**   Taking data from a file and inserting it into a word-processed document. Can be used to send the same letter to lots of different people

**maintenance documentation**   A description of how a computer system has been set up. This will provide information so that alterations or additions to the system can be made easily

**margins**   The positions at which lines of text start and end

**MIDI interface**   The industry standard method of connecting instruments such as keyboards to a computer system

**mixing (sounds)**   Combining different sounds so that they are played at the same time, producing a composite sound

**Modem**  A modulator / demodulator which converts digital data for transmission along telephone lines and extracts the digital data from received signals

**mouse**  A device attached to the computer by a cable, and moved across a mat. The movement rolls a ball inside the mouse and this movement is translated into movement of a pointer on the screen. Selection is by clicking one of the buttons on the mouse

**moving blocks (of text)**  Selecting a whole section of text which is cut out of the document and then inserted somewhere else

**multimedia**  Using sound, pictures, text (and often animated sequences) to communicate information

**network**  A collection of linked computers, able to share resources

**object**  A part of a drawing or page which is handled as if it is a single item

**optical disk**  A disk which uses light to store and retrieve data

**page template**  The layout to be used for all the pages in a document, stored as a file

**painting package**  A package used to produce pictures. The computer stores the colour of each pixel, altering the size of sections is difficult

**password**  A word, or number, which has to be typed into the computer system in order to gain access to programs or data

**password hierarchy**  A system of passwords, giving different levels of access to programs and data

**peripheral device**  A piece of hardware (such as a printer or a sensor) which is connected to a computer

**pitch (of a sound)**  How high or low a sound is

**pixel**  One spot on a computer screen which can be illuminated in a particular colour or left black

**portrait orientation**  Arranging the layout of a page so that the document is tall and narrow

**primary key field**  A database field in which each value is unique, allowing an individual record to be found easily

**printing (files)**  Sending data to a printer to produce output on paper

**procedure**  A set of instructions within a computer program, to carry out a particular task. Each procedure has a name and the task can be carried out using this name

**processing stage**  In a computerised system, this is a stage where data is used or altered in some way

**program**  A set of instructions, in the correct order, which cause the computer to carry out a particular task

**programming language**  The words and phrases that can be used in writing a computer program make up a programming language

**query**  A method used to search a database for records which have certain things in common

**range (of numbers)**  Numbers between a known minimum value and a known maximum value

**range (of cells)**  All the cells in a spreadsheet that lie within an area between two specified cell addresses

**real-time**  A computer application in which input data is processed quickly enough for this data to affect the output from the system

**record**  A record contains data about one person or thing. It is divided into fields

**record area**  The part of a database report which contains data for each record selected for printing

**relational database**  A database in which the data is kept in more than one file. These files can be linked

**report**  The printed output from a database system

**report format**  The layout of a database report

**resolution**  The number of separate points which can be displayed on a computer screen

**right justification**  Arrangement of text, or other data, so that the right hand edge makes a straight line down the page. The left hand edge is not even

**sampling (sound)**  Storing sound data so that it can be played back using the stored data

**sampling interval**  The time between taking samples of data

**saving (files)**   Storing data on a disk or tape so that it can be reloaded later

**scan**   To detect the pattern of light and dark, or different colours, on a page and transmit the data to a computer where it is used to produce a screen image

**scanner**   A device which produces a scan by detecting the amount of light reflected from each point on a page

**search (a database)**   To find all the records in the database which have the required values in certain fields

**selecting (records)**   Marking particular records so that an action applies to all of them. Often done by searching

**selecting (blocks of text)**   Indicating the beginning and end of a section of text which can then be handled using block commands

**sensor**   A device which detects the state of an environmental condition (such as temperature) and transmits a signal to an interface unit connected to the computer

**sequencing (sounds)**   Playing back stored sound samples in a particular order

**Service Provider**   An organisation which provides access to the Internet or other communications facilities

**simulation**   Using a computer model to predict the outcome of particular events. Sometimes connected to a realistic sound, visual and motion effects

**single spacing**   Printing text with no extra space between text lines

**spreadsheet**   A grid of boxes or cells, containing data or formulae, which is used to carry out calculations

**story**   A complete section of text for use by a DTP package

**summary area**   The part of a database report containing data which will only be printed at the end of the final page of the report

**system flowchart**   A diagram showing how data moves through a system

**system specification**   A detailed list of all the tasks a computerised system must be able to carry out, together with any other requirements such as time limits, and amount of data to be stored

**tabs**   Column positions which can be set as required across a word-processed page

**telemetry**   Transmission of data from sensors to a receiving station at a distance

**telesales**   Selling goods by telephoning potential customers

**terminal**   A computer or workstation attached to a network

**testing plan**   A method designed to test a computer system to make sure it works as it should

**text editor**   A simple package used to produce text files. It provides only basic facilities for entering, editing, and saving text

**text file**   A file containing only text. Text files are usually produced using text editors or word processors

**underlining**   Putting a line under a section of text when it is printed

**user documentation**   All the information provided on paper for the user of a computer system

**user guide**   Written instructions telling a person how to use a computer system

**variable**   Something which can change and have different values

**virus**   Code which replicates itself and is transmitted from one machine to another attched to other files. Usually designed to damage data

**white space**   Areas of a page not taken up by text or graphics

**web browser**   Software used to access Internet pages by means of hypertext links

**Wide Area Network (WAN)**   Network in which the computers are linked using communication lines such as phone lines instead of cables

**word processor**   A computer program designed to allow entry, editing, storage and retrieval, and printing, of text

**zoom**   To enlarge a section of a drawing to allow more detail to be included

# Acknowledgements

The authors and publishers would like to thank the following companies, individuals and institutions who gave permission to reproduce photographs in this book:

**Corbis** (10, 114); **Economatics** (116, 122); **Ronald Grant Archives** (35 left, 35 right © Walt Disney Co); ICL Ltd (171, 172)); **Impact** (36, 73); **Lego Dacta UK Ltd** (124); **Science Photo Library** (112 left and right, 113, 121, 123); **Trevor Clifford Photography** (57, 64). Additional photography by Liz Rowe and Ruth Nossek.

We would also like to thank Mr A Hill and Mr B Robinson of Cleveland Educational Computer Centre (CECC), a medical practice in medical practice in NE England, the Urban Traffic Control Department of Cleveland and Mr Woods.

Thanks also to the following bodies who gave permission to reproduce copyright Examination question material:

Southern Examining Group, Midland Examining Group, Northern Examinations and Assessment Board.

The pages were designed by Liz Rowe, who also contributed graphics. Illustrations and graphics by Phil Ford were supplemented by the authors.

# Index